# *You Can* Write a Mystery

GILLIAN ROBERTS

**WRITER'S DIGEST BOOKS**
CINCINNATI, OHIO
www.writersdigest.com

**ACKNOWLEDGMENTS**

Jerry Ludwig and Marilyn Wallace are not only wonderful writers and friends but splendid, careful critiquers as well. Many, many thanks.

Other fine Writer's Digest Books are available from your local bookstore or direct from the publisher.

Visit our Web site at www.writersdigest.com for information on more resources for writers.

To receive a free weekly E-mail newsletter delivering tips and updates about writing and about Writer's Digest products, send an E-mail with "Subscribe Newsletter" in the body of the message to newsletter-request@writersdigest.com or register directly at our Web site at www.writersdigest.com.

07   06   05            7   6   5

**Library of Congress Cataloging-in-Publication Data**

Roberts, Gillian.
  You can write a mystery / by Gillian Roberts.
     p.     cm.
  Includes index.
  ISBN 0-89879-863-9 (pbk.: alk. paper)
  1. Detective and mystery stories—Authorship. I. Title.
PN3377.5.D4Y68   1999
808.3'872—dc21                                                    99-19316
                                                                      CIP

Editor: David Borcherding
Production editor: Michelle Howry
Production coordinator: Kristen D. Heller
Author photo: Robert Greber

## ABOUT THE AUTHOR

Gillian Roberts is the *nom de mystere* taken
by Judith Greber, a former high school
English teacher who has taught writing for
College of Marin, Book Passage, Writer's
Digest and who is currently adjunct faculty
at the University of San Francisco Master's
in Writing program.

Under her own name, she's written four
mainstream novels: *Easy Answers, The
Silent Partner, Mendocino,* and *As Good
As It Gets.*

As Gillian Roberts, she's written over a
dozen anthologized short stories and a mystery series featuring a
Philadelphia high school English teacher named Amanda Pepper.
*Caught Dead in Philadelphia* won the World Mystery Convention's
"Anthony" for Best First Mystery of 1987. Following in the series
are: *Philly Stakes, I'd Rather Be in Philadelphia, With Friends Like
These. . . , How I Spent My Summer Vacation, In the Dead of Summer,
The Mummers' Curse, The Bluest Blood* and *Adam and Evil.* All have
been Mystery Guild selections and translated into Japanese, German
and Danish. Most are available in audio versions from Recorded
Books.

A second series featuring two Bay Area PIs—Emma Howe and her
new trainee Billie August—debuted in 1998 with *Time and Trouble.*

Native Philadelphians, Judith and Robert Greber have been living
in the San Francisco Bay Area for the past seventeen years. They are
the parents of two adult sons.

## TABLE OF CONTENTS

# INTRODUCTION

A prevalent myth has it that the ability to write is innate, almost genetic—like freckles or a predisposition to diabetes. You either have it or you don't, and too bad for you if you don't. This isn't said of the other arts. One seldom hears that people are born opera singers, ballerinas, sculptors, or pianists and therefore voice and music conservatories, ballet masters and art institutes are foolish indulgences.

The truth is, all disciplines have a craft component, skills that enable artists to realize their vision. This includes the art of writing mysteries.

This book offers practical suggestions for handling problems likely to arise during the writing process. These aren't hard-and-fast rules like those for physics, football or international shipping. These are techniques and concepts that can make the going easier. Once you're aware of them, you can use them, break them, realign them or twist them any way you see fit. Whatever works works. We call this form a *novel* because it's there to be reinvented and made new.

There's a world of difference between racing out of control, without a clue as to what we're doing, and expertly racing the Grand Prix, readjusting the rules of the road to suit our needs. Behind the wheel or in front of the computer, you should be able to make decisions in your own best interest and based on more than trial and error. Other writers have been down this road; they've tried and erred and tried again and again. You can profit from their hard-won knowledge.

You don't need to reinvent the wheel in order to race in that Grand Prix.

# 1 GETTING READY

When we think about writing mysteries, we think about plot ideas, characters, clues, and so forth, all of which will be dealt with in later chapters. But none of those items will see the light of day if you don't first resolve issues that can frustrate and subvert your ambition to write a mystery. So please first consider the:

## FIFTEEN COMMANDMENTS FOR MYSTERY WRITERS WHO WANT TO BE PUBLISHED

(Writing commandments on a computer is much easier than carving them in stone, so I've listed half again as many.)

### I. Thou shalt think like a professional starting now.

Writing's an art, but publishing's a business. It's counterproductive to present anything less than your absolute best to an editor. The more editorial time your work requires, the less enthusiasm the publishing house will muster. Learn your craft and become your own first editor.

### II. Thou shalt begin and keep going till you're through.

All beginnings are hard. The beginning of a novel is the hardest part to write. The beginning of each chapter is hard. The beginning of each day's work is hard. Knowing that, grit your teeth and get past those beginnings. Then finish the book. Nothing's more discouraging than an unfinished piece of work. Writing is rewriting. Let that give you confidence as you stumble along—you can and will make it better *after* you finish a draft.

### III. *Thou shalt take your efforts and desires seriously.*

This requires a level of confidence that may be difficult at this stage, but honor your desire. It's important to you—or you wouldn't be reading this book—and it's a worthy, rewarding ambition.

### IV. *Thou shalt call it work.*

Give your labor the dignity of its title. Don't wait till you "find the time." Time wasn't lost—it was differently allocated. Writing time has to be created. Figure out what schedule and frequency is realistic for you in your current life. No law dictates when or how, for how long or by what method one writes—as long as one writes. Negotiate—gently, realistically and specifically—with nearests and dearests who may not instantly understand your need for solitary and protected writing time. Once you have a schedule, stick to it.

### V. *Thou shalt write for yourself, not the market.*

If you imitate whatever's hot at the moment (e.g., serial killers, courtroom dramas, parrot-sleuths), you'll have an unsatisfying year or two rehashing someone else's inspiration and learning next to nothing. Worse, when it comes time to market the book, those killers and parrots and lawyers will be passé. Write what tickles your mind. Write a book you'd love to read.

### VI. *Thou shalt not wait for visits from the muse.*

The Muse is about as likely as Mr. or Ms. Right to show up just because you want her to. If you buy into the "possessed artist" myth, you'll be stymied by the many unpossessed, uninspired moments while writing something as long and complicated as a mystery, and the odds will shift against your finishing your book. Don't wait—get on with your life. (Oddly enough, once the perverse Muse realizes you don't need her, she'll show up.) Inspiration comes with the writing and seldom precedes it.

### VII. *Thou shalt not ask whether you are good enough.*

This is not a valid question. You *are* good enough—or can be. The good (and possibly bad) news is that writing well is a lifelong challenge. The more you do, the more you learn you can do, and the more you then do beyond that. Start getting better at it now.

3

### VIII. *Thou shalt not intimidate yourself by comparing your writing with a published and polished work.*

You never see the awful early drafts of that book you love. Learn from works you admire (later we'll talk about how), but don't let them become stumbling blocks.

### IX. *Thou shalt not worry whether your idea is new enough.*

There are no new ideas in the area of crime, only new voices and approaches to telling us about those crimes and their meanings. Yours is one of the new voices.

### X. *Thou shalt not talk your idea away.*

You're a writer. The words on the page will allow the reader to live your story. If you *tell* it to someone, the experience will be completely different and disappointing. Don't dissipate your energy, imagination and enthusiasm by talking about what you're doing. As they say, just do it.

### XI. *Thou shalt not self-censor at all during the first draft.*

This draft is yours for the adventure of finding out what you think. Future drafts will be for others. Hold off your critical self until those future drafts.

### XII. *Thou shalt not risk writer's paralysis by looking for the precise word or being afraid of sounding dumb.*

Two quotes on my bulletin board are "Don't write it right, write it down" and "We all have a lot of bad writing in us, and it's important to get it out so we can get past it." Get the bad writing out. Fill pages. Move ahead. You'll make it better later on.

### XIII. *Thou shalt not believe that if writing's hard, you must be no good.*

The only people who think writing is easy are people who don't write. Writing's a difficult, courageous act. Bravery is required, as well as a great deal of slogging along. A lot of our work is work.

### XIV. *Thou shalt not set yourself up for failure with impossible goals.*

Don't swear you'll turn out one hundred pages a week or that you'll wake up at three o'clock in the morning and write until six, then tend the baby and get ready for work. Nobody writes a whole mystery: We all write one page at a time. Set reasonable goals and commit to them. If you establish a (reasonable) routine, whatever it is, your subconscious will understand that you'll be back to nourish this mystery again, and it will feed you in return—embellishing and enriching your idea between writing sessions while you live your other life. Make your goal finding out what you can accomplish as a writer at this stage and on this day.

## XV. Thou shalt not believe in writer's block.

Under all the words and mystique spun around it, writer's block is old-fashioned fear: fear of yourself, of others' opinions, of not being good enough or new enough or clever enough. Fear of the critical voice of parents, lovers, teachers or the neighbor who thinks you should spend your free time mowing the lawn. Fear of exposing your secret self and finding it unworthy. Fear, as the man said, of fear itself.

What's to be done about it? See commandment XIII, on writing as an act of courage. Acknowledge that writing makes you vulnerable. No matter that your firsthand experience of murder is nil; that you in no way resemble your protagonist, villain or victim; and that you've never lived in Ancient Crete, where your mystery is set. Even so, your values, which are your real self, are going public via your work, and self-exposure is daring and frightening.

But if you can free yourself to understand that you are complexly human—and so are your readers—and if you put that honest revelation on paper, you'll have a heady, liberating and exhilarating adventure.

That said, you're ready for the trip—ready to apply your rear to a chair, stare down your devils and make words happen until you have a mystery. And ready to enjoy yourself in the process!

# 2 THE BASIC ELEMENTS

Every novel poses a question. Will Ahab conquer that whale? Will John win the hand of Mary? Will Scrooge change in time? The question in a mystery concerns a crime—whodunit? Why'd he do it? Is he going to do it—or do it again? Who is going to do it? The mystery novel is the answer to one, or a combination, of these questions.

You may write about a whole lot more than crime in your mystery. You might illustrate a facet of human nature, explore national issues, reassess historical "truth" or analyze the potential of a scientific discovery. Good for you—you'll have a rich, multifaceted book. But all the same, the crime and its solution remain the book's backbone. Everything else should flesh that out and be related to it.

Because a mystery has a beginning, middle and end (a crime, a search for answers, a solution) and develops logically, it appeals to the innate human need for well-structured stories. By definition it has dramatic conflict—an unsolved crime plus a quest for justice that leads to complications and ever growing tension—and a conclusion that is, in its own fashion, fair and just, so the mystery makes for pleasurable reading. Noir or humorous, hard-boiled or cozy, mysteries are the descendants of morality plays, and in an increasingly complex and ambiguous world, they provide the comfort of the absolutes of right and wrong, good and evil—or at least evil and less evil.

The puzzle mystery provides intellectual stimulation plus the enjoyment of game playing—the contest between the reader, the writer, the sleuth and the villain as to who will first triumph when all are given the same information.

Given all these instinctive and built-in pleasures, the popularity of the genre is no mystery.

For the writer, the genre is a generous one, allowing enormous freedom. The crime can raise social, political or psychological issues in a setting rich with real or imagined historical events and figures. The tone of the book and/or its protagonist can be humorous or deadly serious, satirical or tragic. The detective can be as morosely complex and cerebral as Hamlet or as amused and irritated by life's insanity as a Carl Hiaasen protagonist.

Crime fiction subgenres evolved out of various authors' world views (Is the crime an outrage in an orderly world or just another day's slaughter in the human jungle?) and what they wanted to say about them.

## SUBGENRES: TYPES OF MYSTERIES

In addition to the classic whodunit puzzle, we have mysteries in which we know who did it, but we read on in order to see "whydunit." *The Suspect*, L.R. Wright's Edgar-winning novel, shows us on page 1 who committed the crime and how. *A Judgement in Stone* by Ruth Rendell tells us immediately that a family was murdered because a servant was illiterate, and then it holds us captive as she shows us just what that means. Or the mystery can focus on whether the criminal will get away with it, as in caper novels, where we watch a crime being planned and attempted and the question is whether it will be successful.

For any of these, we can have an amateur sleuth, (including semi-pros—amateurs who work close to crime—such as lawyers, investigative journalists and insurance investigators), a private investigator (PI) or a police officer as our detective. Our milieu and procedure will vary to some extent depending on which we choose, but again, this is not a hard-and-fast rule. The traditional noir American mystery has a PI prowling mean streets, while the British traditional puzzle, or "cozy," is set in genteel villages and vicarages, where (mostly offstage) crime is in no way a normal occurrence. But these days, there are cozy PIs and gritty tales of amateur sleuths.

Subgenres evolved—and continue to do so—from writers' experimentation with this limber genre.

### Suspense

Where the classic mystery investigates something that has already happened, suspense asks the question "What is going to happen?"

In psychological suspense, the possibility of violence or death hovers nearby and will happen unless its secret heart is revealed. Our protagonist—usually an ordinary mortal like ourselves—is, like the detective in the whodunit, seriously tested.

A thriller is a novel of suspense writ larger. More than the girl at the bar or the vicar is at stake. A nation, a legal system or life as we know it on the planet is in a state of risk, as is the brave protagonist who is aware of this. Thrillers can involve espionage, technical terrors, mutant viruses, prehistoric monsters—or lawyers.

In romantic suspense, the emotional life and fortunes of the protagonist may be of equal weight to the mystery and just as filled with problems.

Any mystery, lit from midnight noir to midday bright, can be set at any point in history. It's up to you. If you could time travel (and you can, via writing), what era and locale would you like to explore? Set your crime there.

These forms have crossed over one another and sometimes merged. Few contemporary mysteries are pure puzzles where the detective summons all his suspects into a room and declares one of them the evil-doer. Instead, we most often have a climactic scene of physical confrontation between the detective and the villain. Whatever basic differences once existed between mysteries and nonmysteries have blurred as well. Once a purely cerebral creation with lots of plot and little characterization, the best mysteries today are as fully fleshed as any of their fictional kin. Too often, when a mystery is exceptional, reviewers claim it "transcends its genre." Unfair. Instead, it exemplifies the highest potential of the genre.

## THE "RULES"

The "rules" that govern the mystery are the rules that govern all fiction. Every novel needs suspense and drama.

Every good writer plays fair with his reader and creates a believable world the reader can enter. This means the mystery writer doesn't withhold necessary information from the reader. If the sleuth knows something, so does the reader. (This doesn't mean that our clever sleuth can't make inferences that escape the reader, but even though he can—and will—his deductions shouldn't be based on knowledge so rarified that there's no possible way the reader could have figured it out.)

The writer can't (visibly) manipulate his characters or plot to fit his solution. A villainous creature doesn't suddenly turn pussycat, nor is a crime solved by a sudden illogical coincidence.

## THE SEVEN Cs
In addition to the crime, your mystery—like every other novel—must contain certain basic story elements. For the sake of alliteration, let's call them the Seven Cs: characters, conflict, causality, complications, change, crisis and closure. If your book doesn't have all these, it won't work. Since more specific crime-writing techniques grow out of these concepts, let's look at each in turn.

### Characters
A story happens to and because of someone, so *characters* are a basic ingredient. Your imagined people are so important we'll devote a chapter or two to them later in this book.

### Conflict
The fundamental element of all drama is *conflict*, the clash between what's wanted or intended and what prevents or frustrates that desire. Happily for mystery writers, conflict comes with the territory, because in committing a crime, the criminal defies what the community (the law) wants. In our mysteries, the crime of choice is most often murder because it is the ultimate offense and it therefore produces the most absolute and unequivocal of conflicts. Life vs. death, law vs. order are now in conflict one with the other, and the magnitude of the offense forces action, either in the pursuit of justice for deeds already done or the pursuit of evildoers because of deeds they intend to do.

The basic conflict represented by the crime that moves your story engine is only one of many large and small conflicts that will be in the book. There will be the internal conflicts of what the antagonist wants vs. the status quo; what the sleuth must choose to do given various options, none of them completely satisfactory. There are the conflicts of human interaction—personality conflicts of people with different goals, hostile witnesses, uncooperative co-workers, frustrating red tape. In life, these might produce ulcers, but they produce healthy fiction.

It's best for your story if the two sides of the conflict are equally weighted. Your protagonist should be the mental equal of your antagonist. Otherwise, it's an unfair fight and a rout rather than the difficult quest it should be, and the tension and reader identification will be reduced.

Tension, the charge that keeps those pages turning, comes from the battle between the challenge and the character's need and ability to meet it. He has to do it—but it's so hard. He's repeatedly foiled, but he must keep trying. He cannot, even as an amateur and accidental sleuth, give up and walk away from it. (When you're developing your characters, you'll build in the reason for this compulsion to unravel this particular mystery—his history or psychology.) What the obsessed protagonist wants has to be important. Even if you're writing about the police, pros who have seen and done it all, this crime can't be another routine murder, just another day's work. This one—your story—is an urgent and personal quest.

## Causality

The reasons why the murder happened, why the detective is passionately involved in this case, why his actions produce still more difficulties, are examples of *causality*. The laws of physics apply to fiction—actions produce reactions. Events do not simply happen and hang there. They happen *because* something else happened, and then the reaction to what happened—your detective's behavior—affects still more, including your detective's life. There has to be this internal logic—things happen because other things happened. Even psychotics have reasons, odd though they be, for their behavior.

Not only do bad things keep happening to our good sleuth, but the things that happen keep getting worse and more intense because of pressures being brought upon her (cause and effect again). Because secrets worth killing for are being dredged out of their hiding places, there is even more reason for extreme behavior. Because the investigation shines a light on many people, possibly irrelevant secrets produce still more odd reactions. These may be red herrings, but they have logical cause and effect behind them. Because of all this muddle, the detective becomes more determined to probe and push. Think of your story as a snowball, gaining breadth and heft because of where it's been and what it's picked up along the route.

## Complications

These further problems are called *complications*. The danger the sleuth is trying to prevent grows ever more possible, its threat more serious. The evolving picture of what really happened seems to be clarifying—but the steps the sleuth takes to prevent, explain or end the danger are all only partial solutions. He finally locates the seemingly vital piece of the puzzle—and it turns out to be a wrong lead or only a fragment of a puzzle piece, dragging new questions along with it. The sleuth feels his work is in vain; and the struggle for understanding becomes more intense as time runs out, theories are reworked and the struggle is resumed with still higher stakes.

## Change

With each complication, the sleuth adds a bit of knowledge. The picture of the situation is readjusted; the opinion of a character, altered. We feel in motion as readers because each of these shifts is a *change*, and when we realign our perceptions, we get an almost unconscious sense of motion, of something happening. You could write a nonstop round of fistfights and chases, but if things were the same at the end of them as at the beginning, the reader would feel that nothing much happened.

## Crisis

Eventually, when the complications and changes have produced an increasingly tense situation, we reach a point where, once and for all, one side or the other is going to triumph. This is the *crisis*—the point of no return. It's do-or-die time, often quite literally.

This scene will be the biggest, most dramatic clash of your book. Generally it's a direct confrontation between the sleuth and the villain.

## Closure

And then your story is over, its question answered, and you have a sense of what its significance was. This provides *closure*, one of the great virtues of fiction. We welcome a story's rendering of wrongdoing and evil because we know, unlike in real life, it will ultimately be over and resolved. Things have changed at the end of the story from how they were at its start. The villains have been stopped or acknowledged as unstoppable, the scales of justice momentarily realigned. Ideally, the protagonist's life has also been redefined because of what he learned through this investigation.

# 3 AMATEUR OR PRO, SERIES OR STAND-ALONE

The mystery or crime novel has many variations on the basic theme. Which niche you decide to occupy should most logically depend on which you enjoy reading.

A first consideration is who your sleuth will be. Amateurs, licensed private investigators and police professionals each have strengths and weaknesses.

## THE AMATEUR

The amateur sleuth is Everyman, confronted with a problem that challenges the best of what he's got. That's why readers can strongly identify with the story and ultimately feel reassured that in a world with often overwhelming problems, the street smarts, courage, hidden talents and common sense of an ordinary person can meet life's most challenging demands.

The amateur also affords the writer the chance to explore interesting milieus. Amateur sleuths run the gamut of occupational possibilities, a tiny portion of which include Nevada Barr's park ranger, Annette Meyers's Wall Street headhunter, Barbara Neely's domestic worker, Aaron Elkins's forensic paleontologist, Sarah Andrews's geologist and Abigail Padgett's child welfare worker. You can add texture and interest to your mystery via the idiosyncrasies, pitfalls and opportunities of whatever field you know or are willing to research.

Because this sleuth is an accidental one, thrust into a situation where he must act but isn't professionally prepared to do so, mysteries with amateurs tend, in general, to be closer to the classic puzzle than to the noir, tough-guy mode. Because the protagonist is not necessarily armed and/or physically tough, the story has, in general, less violence. This forces you—and your character—to rely more on quick thinking and improvisation. In lieu of guns or fists, I have had Amanda Pepper use a file cabinet, a car, *Dr. Spock's Baby and Child Care*, and a can of hair spray made into a flamethrower. Nancy Pickard has gotten creative with lingerie, having Jenny Cain use her bra as a garotte in *Generous Death* and her panty hose as a rope in *No Body*.

The amateur sleuth's methodology is not constrained by law, as is that of private investigators and the police. Within the limits of sanity and self-preservation, the amateur can do whatever he must—lie, assume disguises, break and enter. The official law must work within more stringent boundaries.

Although tea cozies and country houses may have nothing to do with your amateur's world, novels featuring a nonprofessional are often put into the "cozy" subcategory. The crime is an outrage, a gaping hole in the social fabric. There is a minimum of overt violence and a maximum of intellectual pyrotechnics, and murder is given its dreadful due as the impact of the crime and its aftereffects are examined.

The flip side of the coin is that you'll have to work hard to justify the amateur's need and opportunity to sleuth. Even though the reader is predisposed to suspend disbelief on this score, you still have to make moonlighting as a detective seem rational. Why aren't the police adequately taking care of this? Why would this citizen choose to face danger?

There are stratagems for getting around this hurdle. Sometimes the sleuth is the prime suspect and has obvious reasons to find the real killer. And even if she isn't in danger because of the way the investigation's going, someone or something she very much cares about must be.

Writing about an amateur character doesn't mean you can be oblivious to official law enforcement. Although you want the police to be misguided or disinterested so that your amateur saves the day, you need to do enough research in the real world to avoid having your amateur's behavior seem ridiculous.

## THE SEMI-PRO

Somewhere between amateurs and professionals are the semi-pros— the journalists, lawyers and insurance investigators who in many ways have the best of both worlds. They have access to and logical involvement with the world of crime, they are protected against being forced to reveal their sources, and they don't have the rules and regulations that govern the behavior of PIs and police. But even with these advantages, make the risk and involvement plausible and necessary—and research the sleuth's actual profession so you keep that realistic base.

## THE PRIVATE INVESTIGATOR

The next category revolves around the archetypical American hero—the private investigator, described by Raymond Chandler: "Down these mean streets a man must go who . . . is neither tarnished nor afraid." Today's PI may be an untarnished woman tooling down suburban streets—with the traditional fisticuffs, womanizing and hard drinking gender adjusted—but reader disbelief doesn't have to be suspended over quite as deep a canyon with a PI as with an amateur sleuth. Readers have immediate interest in these investigators. The PI wears the mantle of a clear-visioned seeker of justice, more iconoclastic than the law, but ultimately on the side of the angels. He (or she) is the ultimate individual, the cowboy-loner, a figure larger than life. By stepping into this tradition, even while making it your own, you also have logic on your side as to why and how this person became involved with an investigation.

Pragmatically, your PI has, if you like, a license to carry a gun, which saves a lot of time in figuring out methods of self-protection.

But do be aware that the "licensed" part of the PIs title involves regulations and prerequisites. Hollywood's clichéd private eye seems to need only a rented office with his name stenciled on the door before he rushes off to find out who murdered John Doe. But Hollywood's home state actually requires that wannabe PI to put in six thousand hours of qualifying investigative experience before being licensed. Research your setting's requirements. Your readers expect and deserve a strong and realistic base to your fiction.

## THE POLICE

Playing by the rules is twice as important if you're writing a police procedural. The strength of this type of mystery is its gritty realism. The writer doesn't have to explain for a second why the protagonist deliberately chases after trouble. Whatever fascination draws us to crime stories is here as a given.

Because a police force is an ensemble, the writer also has the opportunity to develop a world of characters and crimes, both serious and less so, as in Ed McBain's 87th Precinct novels.

But given that any infraction of the police rule book can trash a case so it won't hold up in court—or will invoke a citizen council's wrath—do the research necessary to have that basis of reality, over which your imagination can fly. Find out how the police department is structured and who is able to do what. Find out (and then invent if needed) the way the day or shift is organized. Researching this and other subjects is discussed in a later chapter.

Or you could place your police protagonist in a small town, as Joan Hess does with Arly Hanks in Maggody, Arkansas, and Charlene Weir does with former San Francisco cop Susan Wren, who replaces her dead husband as police chief in a small town in Kansas. In your town, rules can be bent to meet your needs, although it still would be good to have the village police official be aware of how much more latitude he has than he'd have in bigger cities.

There are, of course, further spins on the four broad categories above, including historical mysteries, which may or may not involve government-sanctioned investigators. Among other reasons, as contemporary forensic advances leave less and less to speculation, the freedom of setting a novel in a past that had no official law enforcement and couldn't even identify fingerprints has definite appeal.

## THE RANGE OF TONES

Any of the above sleuths can have the tone that feels right to you, from village genteel to hard-boiled, hard-drinking, tough and isolated PIs to someone in between, like Jerry Kennealy's Nick Polo PI series, which he labels as neither hard- nor soft-boiled, but "al dente." You can use as much humor as you instinctively feel, built on situation and/or character. The amateur sleuth novel lends itself to smiles because its protagonist can be legitimately confused, overwhelmed and innocent of what is really going on. But PIs don't have to be dour and serious like Sam Spade. Robert Crais's Elvis Cole is wry and wisecracking, and Parnell Hall's Stanley Hastings is a laugh-out-loud creation. Big-city police are most realistically going to prefer gallows humor and be more calloused for self-protective reasons, but humor is still possible, although more likely in the small-town eccentric world of the imagination, such as Joan Hess's Maggody.

## STAND-ALONE OR SERIES?

Consider whether you're writing a stand-alone book or the beginning of a series. Sometimes the story itself dictates this—as when your character, by virtue of no longer breathing, can't come back for an encore. More often, it's up to you. Both series and stand-alones have pros and cons.

A series builds reader loyalty. Readers (and, one hopes, writers) enjoy revisiting a sleuth, but a series has a built-in danger of repetition, which can lead to author, if not always reader, boredom. This doesn't have to happen. Since the writer doesn't have to reinvent a protagonist, setting or general tone, he can devote his energies to being inventive with plot and discovering new levels and revelations of the givens. This can mean differently structured stories; different types of plots; secondary characters, ideas and issues; or all of the above and more.

Even dramatic leaps in style or concept are possible. Linda Grant switched from straight first person, past tense to multiple points of view using both present and past tense in *Vampire Bytes*, the sixth book in her Catherine Sayler series. In order to expand Sharon McCone's—and her own—options, Marcia Muller moved this PI out of All Souls Legal Cooperative and onto her own in book fourteen of the series. In good contemporary series, the character, in subtle but real ways, matures and grows with each installment, providing a fresh challenge to the writer each time out and possibly suggesting major stylistic changes. No one need feel constricted.

If you write a stand-alone mystery or thriller, you have every opportunity to develop new characters, locations and situations and to use whatever fictional techniques appeal to you. You can sustain suspense more easily because the protagonist, lacking any future book contracts, may or may not survive this ordeal. But you run the risk of not developing or maintaining reader recognition. Some writers get around this by developing a consistent theme. Mary Higgins Clark can be counted on to write about women in jeopardy, and Dick Francis established his readership with mysteries set in the world of racing.

If you're writing psychological or romantic suspense, you're likely to write stand-alone novels, since otherwise, we'd have a hard-to-believe hero or heroine who is repeatedly put in extreme jeopardy by a crazed someone.

Whichever subgenre or variety of sleuth you prefer, your choice will present challenges, possibilities as large as your imagination and skills and, ultimately, gratification.

# 4 WHERE DO YOU GET IDEAS?

Mystery writers are asked this question all the time. The questioners are either awed by our fertile minds or afraid that we've acquired our murderous ideas firsthand. The only honest answer is, "We get ideas everywhere." The trick is recognizing them.

A mystery contains lots of ideas, but we'll focus here on the core idea around which the crime is built. Nothing new is happening under the plot-idea sun. Story ideas are eternally recycled, adapted and made new via fresh characters and the voice and world view of their author. This means that anything is grist for your mill. Anything that produces interest and emotion in you can be made to do so in a reader and can be the basis of a mystery.

What troubles or intrigues you? What image, situation, issue, news story, person—read about or known personally—infuriates, confuses, frightens, disgusts, amazes or appalls you? What topic keeps coming up in your conversation? Let your passions and concerns be your guides. Even if you don't know precisely how something makes you feel, but you know you can't let go of it, make note of it and let it simmer in an idea file until it finds its meaning.

## HARVEST NEWS STORIES

The daily paper is the mother lode of murderous ideas. Mysteries are about passions run amuck—desire for love, money, power or safety pushed beyond sane confines. News is about what people want and what they do to get it, which means it's filled with potential idea springboards.

Today, during rudimentary desk clearing, I found three news stories I'd recently clipped. One was about an amnesiac woman who'd wandered into a hospital. She thought she knew where she was from, and she gave a married and a maiden name and a date of birth. But no one can find any record of such a person. She troubles me. Why does she think she's this person who seemingly never existed? Why hasn't anyone responded to the AP photo of her? What if . . .?

The next clipping is about a couple who is suing their city. They claim the suicide of their son while in a juvenile detention center was due to problems stemming from his being beaten up on the public transportation system. Because of that, they claim, he turned to drugs and petty crime. Whatever the reality of their situation and the law, this couple's blind despair and need to blame—need to sue—produce the uncomfortable sense of imbalance that means this might be story material. What attracts me will not necessarily attract you. Even if it did, we'd produce different stories, so there is no problem there. Family dynamics interest me more than international intrigue, so I might skip stories about diplomatic impasses that others will turn into best-selling thrillers. *Your* passions will lead to your story.

The third story, from my local paper, concerns the county's recent ban of wild animals in residential zones. No more pet Bengal tigers, alligators, hyenas, venomous snakes, ostriches or Gila monsters, all of which were apparently legal before. My Emma and Billie series is set in my home county, so this might become color—background— or provide a plot or subplot as somebody refuses to part with his monitor lizard. Or it might become the basis of a short story. I don't know which yet, but it's a keeper.

Today's clippings don't happen to include anything from the business section, but that's another gold mine, as are the personals. Or political news. Or the sports section. Or letters to the editor. Or "Dear Abby." Or a feature on a social issue. I've used articles on school censorship, domestic abuse, gamblers leaving their babies untended outside casinos, high school students crucifying a boy who tried to leave a white supremacy group. I've gotten ideas from every section of the newspaper.

## NOSINESS PAYS

The news makers themselves—people—are another splendid source (not, alas, the people who say, "I have a mystery plot for you!"). People telling their stories, gossiping, chatting and looking at life are full of material. Follow your nosiness. Overheard scraps of conversation that leave you wondering what on earth he meant by that or what he could have done to make her so coldly furious with him are ideas. Seeds like these can generate mysteries as you imagine answers. Carry index cards or a small notebook with you, keep a tape recorder in your car, leave a tablet by your bed and record anecdotes that make you cringe, laugh or shake your head in wonderment. Put them into your idea file. Don't trust yourself to remember them.

## CLASSIC PLOTS AND ODD BITS OF INFORMATION

You can also tap the sourcebooks of condensed wisdom about human nature: classic dramas, the Bible, fairy tales and myths. (Julie Smith says each entry in her Edgar-winning Skip Langdon series is based on a myth.) All can be plot springboards. Beginning with sibling rivalry in Cain and Abel's story, going through the jealousy-driven murder in *Othello*, the power-hungry murders in *Macbeth*, the wide-open potential of Faust selling his soul. How about the universal appeal of such fairy tale elements as the Ugly Duckling—and what that wretched childhood did to that duck's psychology when he was a big, strong swan. There's the basis of a lot of revenge stories.

A mystery writer can also build around a surprising fact or bit of knowledge. *Caught Dead in Philadelphia* began when I learned that Winnie the Pooh had another, "real" name, and I wondered if everybody else knew that. If they (including the police) didn't, then couldn't it be a clue a bookish woman might know? I built the woman—Amanda Pepper, English teacher—and a book around it. The core of *The Mummers' Curse* was my visit to the Philadelphia Mummers Museum, where a "frame suit" costume worn in the annual New Year's Day parade was so enormous and structured that I thought a man could be dead inside of it and nobody would notice for a long time. (Once you begin to think like a mystery writer, you do have an unwholesome take on things.) That produced the idea of killing somebody in full view of the spectators during the annual parade.

Many people are sensitive to the ambience of a place, and that's where they begin. They wonder who lives or lived there and what is it about the place that is so gripping.

A character type that intrigues—or infuriates—you is a fine starting point. Use a face sighted across a subway train that suggests a whole life of . . . what? Or someone it's your fortune or misfortune to know. Can we test what intrigues you by making him the sleuth, or squelch what drives you up the wall by making him the victim or the murderer?

I used a real-life model once, borrowing the original's manipulative, deceitful—and charming—ways, although his fictional history was derived from a news story. Irritants can be combined.

Another person's novel, one you wish had gone another route, can be the springboard. I am not suggesting plagiarism, but you can borrow the underlying premise ("a criminal inherits a great deal of money"), make up your own characters and write your own take on it. Update it. Relocate it. Switch genders. What if Butch and Sundance were middle-aged women buddies? Make it your own.

I've even seen the suggestion that when all else fails, the tiny plot summaries in TV listings could be jumping-off spots. Instead of watching the show, work with its premise.

You're not likely to ever find a complete plot start to finish, but building material is everywhere. Often during the writing process, the original news story, person, event or conversation mutates or disappears along with its original meaning and emphasis. That's fine—it was the magnet that pulled in other elements until they, in turn, created your story.

## BEGIN WITH CHARACTER

How do you proceed from that vague bit of something that produces an emotional or intellectual reaction to a plot? If you aren't starting with character, now's the time to move that way. Stories are events that happen to people, so consider the people. You may have already discovered their motives. Say you're using that story about the county ban on wild animals. Could a fictional character care so much about keeping his Bengal tiger that he'd kill for it? Or be killed?

If something you heard or read made you think of a frightening what-if, personalize it. If the what-if is that the world's in danger of ending, who has a chance of stopping the threat? Make it a real test, even for this exemplary person. Give him traits, conflicts or weaknesses that make success difficult. (He will not kill, even in self-defense. He's afraid of heights. He's in a full body cast. She's due to go into labor with quadruplets at any moment.) When an issue or idea intrigues you, consider a character who might be so affected by it that he's driven to crime. Donald E. Westlake's *The Ax*, takes a darkly comic look at what corporate downsizing could mean.

Gather ideas and let them germinate. Happily for all of us, ideas are one resource that isn't endangered.

# 5 DEVELOPING SLEUTHS, VILLAINS AND VICTIMS

A mystery is not what happened, but what happened to a person or people. In order for a reader to care about your plot, he needs to care about your characters, particularly the all-important trio of sleuth, villain and victim.

The fictional impulse to replicate life on the page is based on the idea that everyone is unique and interesting, so always think in terms of specifics. That's what justifies the mystery—the idea that taking an ordinary life is heinous and requires redress.

There are no "typical" people, so aim for the sort of one-of-a-kind person we, and our characters, all are. Amazingly enough, when you create a well-rounded, specific person, often as not, he becomes universal. Think of Christie's Hercule Poirot, Grafton's Kinsey Millhone, Stout's Nero Wolfe, Stevenson's Dr. Jekyll and every other character you remember for a lifetime.

This does not mean that you need total familiarity before you begin your novel. What you need is a good handle on your character. This preliminary stage is like dating your character—you'll ask a lot of questions, gather data and think you know him. The writing phase, however, will be more like the marriage with its many unsuspected revelations as deeper levels of character are revealed through mutual experience. As you both live his adventure you'll learn more, and during the rewriting phase you can make adjustments based on your new knowledge. And if you write a (successful) series, the process will continue as your protagonist evolves and surprises you with new facets of his personality.

## BUILDING FICTIONAL PEOPLE

Fictional people begin life in a variety of ways. Perhaps your plot needs a person terrified of heights, or one foolhardy enough to attempt an impossible rescue. You can begin building someone around that idea. Or your theme might require a certain kind of person to illustrate it. That, too, can be a starting point. Perhaps you've been fascinated (or horrified) by someone, or you've spotted a stranger whose appearance produces an immediate emotional reaction. You back off or feel drawn to him or "know" you'd have nothing in common with him—and you take the time to wonder about the basis of that feeling. You ask yourself about the clues to personality that the person's words, features, gestures or dress produce, and you use what you know of that person to fill in the missing parts.

Most often, your character will be born of a combination of sources, so it's a good idea to carry a notebook or index cards and develop a data bank by jotting down such sightings. Whether you begin from the observed surface and work in or from the interesting psychology and work out—or from pragmatic needs—your next job is to wrap believable life around that starting point.

### Clues and cues to note

Note scraps of real-life dialogue that affect you. You'll probably become aware that you are struck by a gesture or words or dress because its meaning is greater than itself. Make note of what *specific* appearance cues caused you to react emotionally and make immediate value judgments. Don't write the abstract/judgment at which you arrived. Instead of writing sloppy, be specific: "hem unraveling," "stain that looks rubbed at but not removed on lapel," "hair in back matted."

## CREATING A HISTORY FOR YOUR PEOPLE

On and off the page, we are the sum total and end product of our history to this point. A person with a chip—or Mr. Bluebird—on his shoulder wasn't born with it. Something, or a whole lot of somethings, happened along the way.

A character can do anything you like *if* he has a reason and the reason comes out of his history. If he does not act in accordance with the readers' image of who he is, they'll feel manipulated for the sake of plot, and they'll resent it enough to pull back from your story. Plot and character should be twined together, one affecting the other.

You're dramatizing the collision of several people's individual stories, so it's important to have a handle on all your characters. For example, the way people respond to inquiries will depend on who they are—not on your sleuth's need for information. Even innocent people may have secrets or fears that impact what they're willing to say and how they say it.

So here are questions to consider for your sleuth, your villain, your victim and anyone else of significance in your novel. Add any questions that help you decipher the mysteries of personality. Most of this won't end up on the page, but it will affect the landscape of your novel like the hidden bulk of an iceberg, and you should be aware of it. Remember what happened to the *Titanic* when it chose to ignore what loomed below the surface.

If the past, or back story, of any character feels complicated, make a chronological list of when things happened to him, so you keep things in alignment as you write the mystery.

It may feel difficult to use this biography for your villain and get close to him this way, but it's important. Nobody, no matter how evil, could live with the full knowledge that she is worthless and subhuman. We all justify our existence and actions by creating an explanation, a world view of our own. You have to get into the head of your bad guy and hear that justification in order to make him real and understand in what fashion he'd behave.

And just as you're going to search for the human, sympathetic part of the villain, so will you search for the warts of your protagonist. Nobody's perfect—except two-dimensional comic book heroes. We want to identify with your protagonist, but we can't if she's not human.

Be sure to build in any special skills or handicaps you'll need later in your story, but if you are thinking in terms of a series character, try not to limit your options for future adventures. If you really want the challenge of devising a series of adventures for one Siamese twin, go to it, but not until you've given such self-imposed limitations thought. If you want to keep your options open, don't be overly specific about how many siblings your protagonist has or what their various occupations are. A surprise visit from a relative you hadn't concocted till the seventh book can trigger a case. Decide whether you want to make your sleuth part of a couple or leave romantic options open to make the introduction of future dangers and adventures easier.

*Consider the character's . . .*

**Vital statistics:** Name, place of birth, education, current residence, age and state of health.

**Distinguishing features:** Height, weight, physical features, coloring, mannerisms of speech or gesture.

**Background:** Where was he raised? In what way? What were his parents' occupations and value systems? What kind of people were they? Is the character fighting childhood, trying to replicate it, trying to deny it, proving something because of it? Are/were there siblings? What do they do? Are they close?

**Personality:** Is this character: cheerful or depressed? Talkative/silent? Adventurous/cautious? Adaptable/rigid? Placid/worrying? Sociable/reclusive? Extroverted/introverted? Self-confident/insecure? Cooperative/competitive? Careful/careless? Fair-minded or biased? Stoical/emotional? Tidy/sloppy?

**Intellect:** How does he feel about his abilities? What kind of student is/was he?

**Occupation:** How does he/she feel about it? How did he choose this work? What are the rewards and dangers of this work? What mistakes could be made, what could go wrong and what would the consequences be?

**Political and religious beliefs:** What are they and how important are they to this person? Do they involve his joining groups, participating in events or demonstrations or actions, limiting his actions or associates?

**Favorite physical activities:** What are they and what role do they play in his life?

**Special talents or skills:** These may be what enable the sleuth or villain to accomplish his goals.

**Life souvenirs:** Events, objects, friendships and memories that travel through life with him. What is their significance?

**Pets:** Past and present.

**Typical day's routine:** Breakfast through bedtime.

**Leisure activities, including entertainment:** Favorite TV shows, reading material, theater, music.

**Fantasies, daydreams and hopes.**

**Self-made environments:** Decor and style of living and work quarters. Include private spots—what's in and on the night table, inside the refrigerator, medicine cabinet, car trunk, office, desk, purse.

**Sense of well-being:** Aspects of present life that are loved and/or hated.

> **Love life:** How does the character feel about the status quo?
>
> **Perceived failures or triumphs:** What is he most ashamed or proud of?
>
> **Fears and desires:** What does he want—aside from solving or committing this crime? Is something in his personality in conflict with the ability to realize these dreams? This may be anything from a pathological fear of heights (think how much the movie *Vertigo* did with this single trait) to a fear of appearing foolish, which dictates how brave or inquisitive he'll be.

## BEWARE OF THE JERKING KNEE

In creating characters, as in every other aspect of your mystery writing, challenge the knee-jerk reaction. If you immediately feel a character whole and with great familiarity, beware that he isn't prefabricated—someone you've seen on too many TV shows and movies and read about in too many books. Rather than write the standard-issue hard drinking, hard-boiled gumshoe or the bleach-blonde duplicitous dame or the twittery old lady or any of their kin, work on their bios until they become new and intriguing. Make them people worth the reader's time and interest.

Decide whether it might help to build in a Watson for your Holmes. Not that the former will do the active sleuthing, but does your sleuth need a sounding board? A confidante? A different sensibility who can help the often solitary protagonist think things through?

Don't forget the victim. Depending on what sort of mystery you're writing, he can be sympathetic or detestable. If everyone hated him it is, of course, easier to create a wide list of suspects. On the other hand, if nobody hated him, you have an interesting extra spin to your mystery, and your protagonist's quest to find answers seems more urgent. And even if everyone hated him, don't forget that somewhere, to someone, his loss causes pain. The more complex your victim was, the more complex your novel can be, because the search will lead in more directions.

## THE TRAP OF USING REAL-LIFE MODELS

Beware of basing characters on people you know. Whether you adore or despise the original, you run the danger of writing an unbelievable character. And you limit your possibilities to those offered up in real life. As a fiction writer, you must think of real life—the one that isn't on the page—as no more than a starting point.

Human beings are too complicated and unfocused for writers to replicate, so what you aim for is your interpretation of a person. Know that your vision is skewed. Don't presume to be omniscient; presume to be a fiction writer. Don't duplicate or try to report; create something new.

Generally, what intrigues you about the person you want to use as a model is his personality or emotional core. Keep that, therefore, and systematically and drastically alter the externals. Change hair or size or gender or the setting in which he must act. Take part of one person and part of another. Does she really have to be a mother even if yours was the model for this rotten person? Could she be a despicable teacher or minister? Does the character have to be a female as long as the unreliability or coldness is there?

If *you* are the original, be doubly careful. "Know thyself" is nifty advice, but it's almost impossible, on or off paper. "Love, defend and justify yourself" is closer to reality, and your writer self won't be aware of all the times you'll censor possibilities and hobble your mystery. You don't have to be on the page as a character because you'll already be on the page in every decision the protagonist makes, in the underlying morality of the world you create, in your sense of humor and tragedy, in your creativity.

Making changes wherever possible—externals, background, occupation—also guards against hurting feelings, losing friends and facing potential lawsuits. People may not recognize their personalities or behavior patterns, but they certainly react to a character with their stats, hair color or occupation.

Exorcizing our demons is a potential bonus of mystery writing, so who better for your victim than that person who has been a thorn in your side? But remember that your reader in Peoria doesn't know what a rat your ex-husband is, so you have to invent a rat she can hate. You can't rely on her having the same emotional reaction you have to the very mention of his habit of licking his lips. Make him up all over again, give him a new irritating tic so that you have to react anew, and you'll be more likely to get it down on paper and to make your point and meaning clear.

## WHAT'S MY CHARACTER'S STORY?

Tell yourself a story about the person you're creating. "He was born nine months after the Woodstock festival to a teenager with no idea who his father was . . . ." "She's fortyish, uncomfortable with intimacy, living alone in an immaculate townhouse . . . ." "Her father was a 'displaced' worker who spent his days mourning his lost status, like the Russian aristocracy in Paris after the Revolution, except her father didn't have the money to buy the beer to cry in . . . ."

If all this seems an unnecessary amount of work, remember that in our nonfictional lives, when we meet somebody new, we're apt to ask, literally, "What's his story?" From people's stories we create an image of who they are, develop a sense of knowing or understanding them, and care about them.

One other thing we ask, of course, is the new person's name. Naming your characters is often amazingly difficult—more like finding, rather than creating, the right name. A name-your-baby book can be a great help. In choosing, remember that names can suggest social class, social aspirations and age. Avoid overusing the same first initial. Even though Velma, Veronica and Victor do not sound alike, the preponderance of Vs will confuse the reader. Make an alphabetical list of every name in your book and try to keep same-sound names to a minimum.

The more you know about your characters, the more they'll return the favor by helping you write your mystery, suggesting inventive, believable and surprising plot turns. (When writers say, "The character made me do that—I had no idea!" it is not generally because the writers are insane, but because they've come to know that imaginary person and understand what that person would and would not do.) So when your character balks at a plot turn and insists on going in another direction, trust him. Don't be rigid about your outline or plans. Try this new idea.

On the other hand, if you absolutely must have that plot turn and it does not fit this man, go back and reconsider the character. Think about somebody else who wouldn't balk at that juncture and might be better for the job.

Get to know the children of your brain. It's well worth the effort.

# 6 WHERE IN THE WORLD WILL YOUR WORLD BE?

The crime, criminal and justice seeker you've created do not exist in a void.

A mystery is a novel in which the world has been disrupted so intolerably that adjustment and accommodation are impossible. The fact that the world and the offense against it cannot coexist is the basic conflict of your mystery and the tension driving it. Therefore, both the crime—the disruption—and the social fabric it shreds need roles in your novel.

Setting is infinitely more than the grass or concrete on which your people put their feet. Setting can, in fact, be the equivalent of another character, and in order to fully envision it, you can write another bio—this time about your place—giving its:

- Map (What's the general terrain? Where are parks, highways, neighborhoods?)
- Buildings, if any (Are there stores, and if so, what sort? Libraries? Services available?)
- Weather
- Transportation (What sorts are there? Is it a problem?)
- Population density
- Economic level
- Ethnic mix
- Crime level
- Traditions, mores, sense of community

Where do the protagonist, villain and victim live and work within that place? What are the physical properties of these places? How do the characters fit into and/or view all these things?

At the very least, your setting provides mood, and it limits or delineates the characters' options and mobility. Consider this description from Dennis Lehane's *A Drink Before the War*:

> Wickham is not an upwardly mobile community. It's dingy and gray as only a mill town can be. The streets are the color of a shoe bottom, and the only way to tell the difference between the bars and the homes is to look for the neon signs in the windows. The roads and sidewalks are uneven, the tar cracked and pale. Many of the people, especially the workers as they trudge home from the mills in the dying light, have the look of those who've long ago gotten used to the fact that no one remembers them. It's a place where the people are grateful for the seasons, because at least they confirm that time is actually moving on.

Compare this with Joan Hess country, specifically *Martians in Maggody*, set in a less-than-flourishing spot which also defines and delineates the characters' lives, but in a completely different tone:

> Outside on the streets (the street, anyway) of Maggody, Arkansas, the sun was shining and the weeds were swaying in a warm breeze. Across the way a goodly number of the 755 residents were going in and out of Jim Bob's SuperSaver Buy 4 Less, and the Suds of Fun Launderette was doing a steady business as spring cleaning got under way. The bench in front of the barbershop was lined with grizzly old coots chawin' tobacco and gossiping worse than the Missionary Society. . . . Rumor had it that rooms had been rented recently at the Flamingo Motel out back, but the molting neon sign still read: V CAN Y, and Ruby Bee was too diplomatic to confirm anything.
>
> This isn't to say that three-quarters of the buildings weren't boarded up or that the merchants were getting rich, but it was a pleasant change after a cold, hard winter that dragged on until cabin fever was epidemic. . . .

Sometimes, as with Tony Hillerman's Navajo mysteries; the Alaska-based mysteries of Sue Henry, Dana Stabenow and John Straley; or Nevada Barr's park ranger series, the setting itself provides plot possibilities. The same murder in a closed, rarified world such as Agatha Christie's placid St. Mary Mead will produce a different set of reactions and behavior than it might in Chicago's South Side.

Wherever you choose to set your story, make it *your* place. Even in the most familiar of settings—or perhaps especially in such places— look with fresh eyes, feel its impact on your viewpoint character, and write as if it were brand new.

This is how Michael Connelly's character Harry Bosch describes Los Angeles in *The Black Echo:*

> Bosch . . . looked through the cleft of the hills to the city below. The sky was gunpowder gray and the smog was a form-fitted shroud over Hollywood. A few of the far-off towers in downtown poked up through the poison, but the rest of the city was under the blanket. It looked like a ghost town.

An image with gunpowder gray, form-fitted shroud, poison, ghost town. That's an attitude.

Sarah Shankman's character, Sam Adams, paints the initial setting of *Digging Up Momma* through its significant details—its atmospheric conditions:

> Come August, nowhere in the Deep South is suitable for woman or beast, but south Louisiana is particularly brutal. Walk out of the air-conditioning, it's like hitting a wet electric blanket turned all the way to ten. Even this early in the morning, the air was steaming, filled with the perfume of swamp and rot and finny creatures. Sam found it a struggle merely breathing, much less loading a car. . . .

Your setting is a powerful instrument to help create the emotional climate of your story. It can also be part of the action, necessitating choices and plot turns, and it can enhance characterization. Use it the way you use any other element, because it needs to be there for the meaning of the story—for its atmosphere—to keep us from feeling as if we're literally drifting through space unmoored. Use it as well to map the story, to let us know where we've moved, how far we've moved, how far we still have to go. Use it for emotional information— for how we should feel about it. The same room can be imposing, forbidding, luxurious or extravagant depending on whose eyes view it and under what circumstances. Don't resort to clichés. A "dark and stormy night" with Frankensteinian lightning flashes to strike terror is a cliché. (A light and stormy night would be interesting, however.) Rain doesn't necessarily mean misery; sunshine doesn't necessarily mean joy. In fact, playing against expectations by having something odious, like murder, in a pretty setting adds to the tension and emotional impact.

Whatever the weather or the man-made or natural setting, see it freshly through the eyes of your characters—and then show it. Don't give us value judgments, like telling us it's gaudy or ugly or pathetically poor. Show it to us via your character's perceptions and reactions.

It may help to borrow a cinematic technique. At the start of a book or a scene, just as during the start of a film while the major credits roll, show enough of the setting to alleviate anxiety. Imagine, instead, a film that opens with voices coming out of fog. We'd feel as if we were in a fun house—blinded, groping and dislocated with no sense of solid ground or walls. Unless that's the precise effect that you want or your protagonist is experiencing, provide the literary equivalent of that establishing shot at the beginning of your novel, so that your reader isn't ignoring your story as he mutters, "Where *am* I?"

If you use the setting for emotional information—for the slant the character has on the room or world—it will also characterize your character and, ideally, create a sense of tension as well, as Julie Smith does at the start of her *House of Blues*:

> In New Orleans, as in many American cities, crime is Topic A. The annual murder rate is somewhere around 400 and climbing. In addition, 2,000 people who do not die are shot each year.
>
> The detectives assigned to Homicide say there are no fistfights anymore.

We're in a setting, but also in a situation—one fraught with danger and tension.

For a different sort of tension, here's Susan Dunlap's Berkeley cop, Jill Smith, at the beginning of *Sudden Exposure*:

> If you can't enjoy the peculiarities of your fellow citizens, you'd better not live in Berkeley. Certainly you should not be a police officer there.

31

I love Berkeley, and the "Only in Berkeley" events that pop up as a regular feature in the press.

Like the daffodils already in bloom, some of our protests are annuals, and some, like the flowering plum blossoms, are perennials. And some—I've exhausted my knowledge of horticulture—flash and are gone.

And here, from Shelley Singer's *Searching for Sara*, is the same place—Berkeley—but not the same place after all because of the different spin she's given the same eccentricities:

Berkeley's a small city, but its neighborhoods range from crack-deadly to urban upscale, from iron-gated groceries to gourmet ghetto.

A precarious balance is somehow maintained, better than in bigger, miles-deep Oakland next door. A balance between the political heritage of the town, which gets in the way of common sense as often as it actually accomplishes anything, the dirty realities of modern urban life, and the cultural multiplicity and richness and excitement any city kid needs to keep breathing.

All three settings are given a unique personality and the potential for trouble. They work to help drive the story.

Whether you've invented your setting or you're using an actual city setting, keep elements consistent by making a map. That way, the memorial fountain in the center of the square won't abruptly relocate itself, something your readers will note with discomfort.

## THE EMOTIONAL DETAIL WORK OF SETTINGS

Look around your current setting—wherever you are reading this—and choose details you'd use to show that you, the character, feel comfortable. Is this a place where good things happen, or is it dangerous, frightening, unfamiliar and intimidating? I'm looking at my computer now in my office, which is cluttered with notes and rough drafts, a cup of tea, a cat on the chair next to mine, and a box full of untended mail on the desk. A bleak February sky lurks outside the window. Do I think of the computer and the clutter as familiar, comforting and enticing signs of work in progress or as threatening signs of disorganization and undone work? Is the drab weather depressing or a fine excuse to stay indoors and move ahead on a project? Am I afraid that cat hair will destroy my computer? What I focus on and what value I give it depends not as much on its reality as on my inner reality, the prism I see through.

What aspects of your landscape do you choose to emphasize? Consider more than the physical objects around you. Include less tangible aspects such as weather, light, temperature, time of day, season.

Don't think of your setting as description to be laid in great rhapsodic blobs. Description is not action. Description is fictional cholesterol, clogging your story's lifeblood. Elmore Leonard's wise dictum is: "Leave out the parts people skip."

*Use* setting in the action, dialogue and characterization so we get an emotional reading of it, so it works in the total piece of fiction. If it's been raining, have your character's trousers splashed by a passing car as he tries to cross the street. Make that offense add to the frustrations of his day.

Make architectural or pastoral detail work by letting us know what effect it has on the scene, the mood, the characters and their actions. In essence, any description should be loaded or slanted or colored to achieve an effect. It doesn't have to be an exotic effect, but it should work for the whole story and what you're trying to convey and, as much as possible, be a part of the ongoing action.

Give a strong overview (that establishing shot) and a few significant details and move on, adding more details later as they work for your story. Your characters are moving through this environment. Use the parts they'd use or notice or stumble over. Here's a historical example from Margaret Lawrence's *Hearts and Bones* that gives us a sense of the mores and customs of the Revolutionary Era in which Hannah, a midwife, lives:

> Hannah . . . scrubbed at a smudge of ash she had left on Jennet's cheek. Then she turned to Julia. "That baby of Rugg's must be impatient of our arrival, Aunt. Shall I saddle Flash, or will you walk today, as I do?"
>
> "I shall ride, of course. And sidesaddle, too, as you ought to do yourself, instead of wading through the snow in those old clothes like a hoyden!" Julia stood up and took her niece's face between her two hands. "You fly in the face of convention once too often, and it will turn and bite you!

33

Must you always be giving old biddies like Mistress Kemp an excuse to cluck at you? Come, at least wear a cap to Mrs. Rugg's."

Hannah extracted herself from the old lady's embrace and marched off to get her cloak and boots. "No, Aunt-dear," she called over her shoulder. "You must pardon me. A cap doesn't suit me. Let them cluck as they please."

## REMEMBER WHAT YOU SET UP

Refresh our sense of place throughout your novel. Remember to keep your characters somewhat aware of where they are. Even a familiar room will be noticed anew when something is wrong, upsetting or threatening. If it's humid and hot at the beginning of a scene or novel, keep the temperature up throughout. Have clothing stick to bodies; people mop foreheads, feel lethargic, thirsty and prone to searching for shade or air-conditioning. If you remember where you are, so will the reader.

Weather conditions can affect people's moods and tempers, foreshadow action and raise tension as in the famous beginning of Raymond Chandler's story "Red Wind":

> There was a desert wind blowing that night. It was one of those hot dry Santa Anas that come down through the mountain passes and curl your hair and make your nerves jump and your skin itch. On nights like that every booze party ends in a fight. Meek little wives feel the edge of the carving knife and study their husbands' necks. Anything can happen.

There is no rule as to what details to pick. Think, however, of what makes the place unique and what the purpose of the environment is.

Try to get texture, shape, style, color, pattern, movement onto the page. Don't limit descriptions of setting and atmosphere to purely visual terms, and don't make them stagnant. Instead of having the sun "come out," show its effect with telling details (colors change, shadows happen, temperature rises).

If you're using a real city, by all means include local landmarks and scenic spots. Readers love to recognize where the action is happening. Just make sure you have it right—that a person could get from A to B in that time or manner. Even in real cities, I invent names of businesses in which people commit crimes. It's easier, dates the book less, and avoids potential lawsuits. I'd use a real site if it were a civic or historical building because it seems to be public property—mine, too.

Beginning writers often stall on the issue of logistics—how to move a character into and out of a setting. The sense is of moving mountains, not mere mortals. But again, another joy of fiction is the ability to skip the boring parts. If the leave-taking does not have plot or emotional significance (as would a teary farewell or an escape from a locked room), leave it out. Begin your scenes with the character already in the room. End the scene when its purpose has been fulfilled. Begin the next one wherever you want it, with a line establishing the time that's elapsed or how difficult it was to get there. Here's how Marcia Muller got her protagonist, Sharon McCone, from San Francisco to Oakland in *Till the Butchers Cut Him Down*:

> "Come on." He started toward the waiting JetRanger.
>
> I hesitated, then followed. There was a definite danger in associating with Suits: what if he succeeded in training me not only to refrain from asking questions but also to take orders?
>
> [double space]
>
> "It happened approximately the way Mr. Gordon described it to you."
>
> I caught a note of reserve in Dick Farley's voice and glanced up at the manager of the Jack London Terminal on Oakland's Inner Harbor. . . .

An efficient ride not only over the bay, but right into the significant action of the next scene.

# 7 A POINT OR TWO ON POINT OF VIEW

Through whose eyes do you want to see your story? Do you want the reader to see only what your detective apprehends or do you want him to see, firsthand, the victim, villain and detective on a collision course? Do you want the reader to view your character from outside ("he opened the door slowly, his hand trembling") or be inside of him ("I could barely turn the doorknob, my hand shook so violently").

Point of view is simply the vantage point from which the reader sees your story.

## THIRD-PERSON POINTS OF VIEW
If you were literally instead of figuratively eavesdropping on your characters, you could put listening and viewing devices on the ceiling of every room, the branches of every tree and the roof of every car the character visited. We call this *third-person point of view*, and with it, we observe what the character does.

### Objective point of view
If the "microphones" are all outside the character, we have the literary equivalent of a movie—everything seen and heard from outside. This objective point of view is the one Dashiell Hammett uses in *The Maltese Falcon*. Look at how external Sam Spade's reaction is to being asked if he'd killed his partner:

Spade stared at her with bulging eyes. His bony jaw fell down. He took his arms from her and stepped back out of her arms. He scowled at her and cleared his throat.

She held her arms up as he had left them. Anguish clouded her eyes, partly closed them under eyebrows pulled up at the inner ends. Her soft damp red lips trembled.

Spade laughed a harsh syllable, "Ha!" and went to the buff-curtained window. He stood there with his back to her looking through the curtain into the court until she started towards him. Then he turned quickly and went to his desk. He sat down, put his elbows on the desk, his chin between his fists, and looked at her. His yellowish eyes glittered between narrowed lids.

"Who," he asked coldly, "put that bright idea in your head?"

We see everything as a camera would. In fact, this could be a script. This viewpoint forces the writer to show, not tell, and to avoid sentimentality; for those reasons writing in the objective point of view is a good exercise to try. But it also leaves out the distinguishing feature of fiction—the ability to read people's minds and hearts. You decide if the trade-off is worth it.

Here's a less literary passage done objectively:

George pulled open the drawers of a chest inlaid with pale and dark woods. He shook his head, then slammed the drawers shut, moving now to the closet, congested with long garments. He patted them down, one by one, then pulled over a chair and examined the contents of the shelf above the dresses. He climbed down. Then he paused, turned and lifted the lid of a lacquer chest on the marble counter. He took a step backwards, hands up.

Still in third person, we'll move one of our listening devices closer to the character, so that we can overhear his thoughts, feelings and sensations, which are italicized:

George pulled open the drawers of a chest inlaid with pale and dark woods. He shook his head, then slammed the drawers shut, moving to the closet, which was congested with long garments. *Old-fashioned dinner gowns, he thought.* He patted their *soft sides* down, one by one, then pulled over a chair and examined the contents of the shelf

37

above the dresses. He found nothing, and climbed down, *feeling defeated. Then he remembered the lacquer chest. She'd pushed it to the back of the marble counter when she realized he was looking at it, as if to protect it from him.* It was unlocked, and he opened it, *expecting nothing.*

*It was as if it leaped out and punched him.* He took a step backwards, hands up, as if to ward something off.

*She'd lied, he thought. After all they had. Sourness filled his mouth. It tasted like her lies.*

### Close third

The device can be clipped to the character's earlobe, and being so close, we can actually hear his thoughts and feel his emotions, often without needing the words *he thought* or *he felt*. This is *close third*, and it has many of the characteristics of first person, the most intimate option.

George pulled open the drawers of a chest inlaid with pale and dark woods. He shook his head, then slammed the drawers shut, moving now to the closet. *Clogged with old-fashioned dresses. Long. Dinner gowns, they called them.* He patted them down, one by one, *smelling mothballs and old age on them.* Then he pulled over a chair and examined the contents of the shelf above the dresses, found nothing, and climbed down, *defeated, until he remembered the lacquer chest she'd pushed to the back of the marble counter when she realized he was looking at it.* It was unlocked, and he opened it, *expecting nothing.*

*Sweet Jesus*! He took a step backwards, *barely able to breathe*, hands up, *warding off something he didn't want to identify. She'd lied. He couldn't believe it. Lied, after all they had. Had never once told the truth. A sour taste filled his mouth.*

## FIRST-PERSON POINT OF VIEW

In first person, we pull down all those external mikes and bugging devices and instead implant a chip inside the character's brain that directly broadcasts his words, actions and thoughts. This is the "I" voice, and nothing is seen from outside the narrator's point of view.

I searched the chest of drawers. Nothing. I wanted to quit right there, let go of it, but I couldn't let it be that easy for her. The closet, then. More of her grandmother's musty garments, preserved in plastic, as if the old lady might rise from the dead and dress for dinner. Always made me laugh when I saw that in thirties movies. I thought that only happened in Hollywood, in films, but here it was. I patted them down, one by one, and still, nothing. Then I pulled over a chair and checked the shelf above the dresses. What a pack rat she was, but in all the mess there was still nothing, so I climbed down, defeated.

Then I remembered the lacquer chest—remembered how she'd pushed it to the back of the marble counter when she realized I was looking at it, as if she was protecting her damned dinner gown family from me.

The chest was unlocked, and I opened it, expecting to be disappointed again.

I was anything but. I put my hands up, as if to ward off something, although I couldn't say what. She'd lied. Never once spoken the truth. I gagged as a foul taste filled my mouth.

First person has many advantages, including verisimilitude. This is our natural way of telling a story: "This is what happened to me, and I was there." The reader is therefore predisposed to trust this narrative, to believe in the storytelling voice as a reality.

However, this means you may never violate the idea that you are inside the character. You couldn't, for example, write "I searched the chest, a frown contorting my mouth" because the character doesn't see that frown. Remember, instead, that you're living inside the character, who can feel muscle movement, so you'd write "Every muscle in my face tightened and pulled down."

First person is the traditional point of view for PI novels (but there's always an exception, as with *The Maltese Falcon*) and a fine point of view for any mystery because the reader can only know what one person knows, so the confusion, fear, suspense and worry of the mystery itself can be made palpable. This is the good news. The bad news is that your plot options narrow. You need to create ways to maintain suspense and mystery and yet have your detective find out things that happen in his absence. This is possible, but not easy, and accounts for (but doesn't excuse) desperate ploys such as the conveniently overheard telephone conversation, the misplaced letter telling something vitally important, and the I-must-explain-my-evil-deeds finale in which the villain fills in all the plot gaps a first-person narrator couldn't know.

This voice also lessens suspense because it's obvious the narrator has lived to tell the tale.

First person is definitely a way to give your detective a unique sound, world view and opinions. The downside is the possibility of your detective's preaching his views too much, so beware.

The first-person narrator is most often the detective or, in a suspense novel, the person in peril. But now and then a secondary character narrates—even though this risks distancing us from the story and lessening the tension—as when Dr. Watson relates Sherlock Holmes's brilliant deductions and wisecracking Archie Goodwin does the same on behalf of Nero Wolfe. These narrators work because the sleuths are so bright that the middleman sensibility is needed between them and the reader. Both these sleuths are also pathologically sedentary men; the stories would include nearly nothing but brain gear whirling if Holmes or Wolfe narrated their own stories while sitting at home and ruminating.

## SINGLE OR MULTIPLE POINTS OF VIEW

Sir Arthur Conan Doyle could have stayed with third person, but he used multiple third-person points of view—Holmes's and Watson's and maybe Moriarty's, too. Third person allows the author to widen the scope and increase tension, which is why it's the technique used by many thrillers. By showing opposing forces heading for collision and having the reader know more than the sleuth, the tension is upped.

Ask yourself how much you want us to know. Is it necessary that we be anywhere except on the trail of the bad guys? If so, consider multiple points of view.

Is your story so complex—building on two continents or in two locales, for example—that it needs more than one set of eyes in order to eventually braid its skeins together? Do you want to build tension by having us inside the mind of your killer in a novel of suspense? Do you want to also show the well-meaning but slow moving forces of good trying to rally against him before he strikes again? And do you want to put your readers on the edges of their seats by also moving to the killer's prospective victim as she decides to—just this once—accept a stranger's offer of a ride just after we've read the odd thoughts of a man driving a car, looking for a girl? . . .

Using multiple points of view also allows for cliff-hangers as we leave one character in a difficult situation and switch to another. Tension is increased because, as in the example above, your reader knows more than any one character knows (although not enough to figure out the entire story until you want her to). But that can make structuring the story complicated, because you don't want the reader to feel as if you aren't playing fair—but neither do you want the reader to know so much that the tension is dissipated.

In order to keep a novel with multiple points of view in focus, give your readers a strong sense of your main character so they can identify with him.

Given that each one of your richly imagined characters has his own hopes, fears, anxieties, secrets and grudges, you'll get a different set of perceptions and actions depending on whose point of view you use.

## OMNISCIENT POINT OF VIEW
One traditional third-person option that should be handled very carefully, if at all, is the old-fashioned omniscient point of view, in which the author can go anywhere in time and space and can be in any character's mind. This point of view option distances the reader. We can't identify with anyone because the God-like author is talking about "those people," leading us around, telling us what they think and what they can't know. Here, I've put in bold print the parts that are not in George's point of view, but presented by an intrusive, outside sensibility.

George, **duplicitous and two-faced as always, left innocent Millicent sitting downstairs, sewing and dreaming of her fiancé** while he, upstairs, pulled open the drawers of a chest inlaid with pale and dark woods. **Although neither he nor she was aware of it, Millicent would have had the last laugh because her dresser drawer had false sides, its real secrets hidden behind them,** so George saw nothing of significance and **did not dream he was being duped.** He shook his head, then slammed the drawers shut. **George was always short**

41

**of temper, an inborn flaw shared by so many of his family
that not one of them recognized it as such.**

This version is full of value judgments and outside opinions, and
the narrator knows what's going on both upstairs with George and
downstairs with dreaming Millicent. And the narrator knows what
neither knows—that the false sides of the drawer are frustrating
George.

This is the voice and point of view used by most nineteenth-century
novelists, but since then, we've moved ourselves offstage so that the
reader is less aware of a storyteller and more deeply involved in our
imagined world. Accidentally intruding in your story is, in fact, a
pitfall to beware. It yanks the reader out of the point of view as well
as out of the illusion that what he's reading is real.

It should be obvious that much of the mystery, not to mention the
idea of playing fair, would disappear with a truly omniscient narrator
because the only way for him to play fair would be to announce on
page 1 what had happened, to whom and why, and end the mystery
right there.

We do still use a form of omniscience today, in third-person single
and multiple points of view, but we use it for presenting settings,
particularly that initial establishing shot which may begin with a pan-
oramic view before honing in on a character's point of view. We use
it for objectively describing events, but we don't interject opinions,
which is blatant telling. Instead, we try to show, through significant
details, the factors that will shape those opinions in the mind of the
reader.

The writer also gives himself access to the mind of one or more
characters, presenting each as fully as possible, but without telling us
more than each character knows, and without making any judgmental
pronouncements about him, so that we can grope our way to the truth
along with the character.

## MANIPULATE SEVERAL POINTS OF VIEW

In order to keep the reader living the story through the viewpoint
character, even if you are using multiple points of view, the least intrusive way to do this is to stay with one pair of eyes for a scene or a
chapter. Then, after leaving a double space to indicate a change of
some sort, in the next segment—even if it's taking place in the same

room and is a continuation of the preceding scene—you can be inside someone else's head. Stay there through that scene until you indicate to the reader that you've again switched to another point of view. Phillip Margolin does this in *Gone, But Not Forgotten*. Below is the end of a scene in which we're in Martin Darius's point of view. The next scene opens (after a section break) in Russ Miller's point of view. Notice how quickly Margolin lets us know we're in a new sensibility.

> The man laughed at his little joke, turned his back and left the bar. Darius watched him go. He did not find the joke, or anything else about the man, amusing.

> A hard rain hit the windshield. Big drops, falling fast. Russ Miller switched the wiper to maximum. The cascade still obliterated his view of the road and he had to squint to catch the broken center line in the headlight beams.

Switch to new eyes only when the new viewpoint adds something vital to your story. Otherwise, show as much as possible through actions, reactions and dialogue.

Sometimes, when a book isn't working, it's a matter of the wrong viewpoint voice. I wrote two thirds of *Caught Dead in Philadelphia* in third person before I "heard" Amanda Pepper telling her own story, and something that had been amorphous and strained eased into itself. On the other hand, when I began my second series, I wanted to contrast the different personalities of PIs Emma Howe and Billie August and play with their misperceptions of each other. And I also wanted the freedom to "be" other characters and clients who'd occupy their lives. So there was never any doubt in my mind that *Time and Trouble* would be in multiple third-person points of view.

You will most likely have an instinctive preference for either first or third person, and as long as it works for the scope of your mystery, go with it. If, along the way, you find that it isn't working, experiment with other vantage points. It's like looking at your story through a kaleidoscope. Turn it this way and that until you find the view that pleases you the most and feels like a fit.

## HELP THE READER UNDERSTAND WHAT YOU'RE DOING WITH POINT OF VIEW

Linda Grant made a dramatic viewpoint switch in her sixth Catherine Sayler book, *Vampire Bytes*. Although the first five books were told in first person, in order to tell this particular story, Grant alternated between Catherine's first-person point of view and several third-person points of view. In addition, she switched from Catherine's past tense narrative to present tense for the third-person segments. Here's the end of chapter one, told through Catherine's viewpoint:

> I didn't look at my watch, so I don't know what time it was. But it must not have been too long before the game in Palo Alto turned deadly, and role-playing became the only way to survive for a girl not much older than Molly.

. . . and here's the start of chapter two, where we're in a different place and sensibility.

> Ben Minor turns left, pauses, then tries to go back, but it's too late. A ball of fire speeds toward him until it fills the computer screen and a maniacal laugh echoes mockingly from the speakers. The screen goes black, then lightens to show a grave with his character's name on it.
>
> "Awright," he says, particularly pleased with the leering skeleton on the tombstone. He took it from a book of photos of old graveyards in New England. "Bones with attitude," he calls it.

Grant establishes what she wants to do early on, and it works. Once you find your viewpoint(s), you should also establish it with the reader. If you're in first person for 150 pages, to suddenly shift to third person will be disruptive and pull your reader out of the story. If you intend to alternate third-person points of view among several characters, establish that by having a "sampler" relatively early. That is, have a chapter in one character's point of view and then another in a second character's viewpoint. That prepares the reader, who will then relax and expect such switches.

Having in essence said, "This is the point-of-view structure I've chosen for this story," maintain whatever you've established throughout the mystery. If you've chosen multiple viewpoints, this doesn't mean that you have to regularly alternate certain voices or follow any rigid pattern; only that you do have to remember we're seeing this tale through more than one set of eyes, so we'll expect to return to that other set from time to time.

44

# 8 PLOTTING, OR LEARNING TO THINK BACKWARD

It's said that Whistler, the artist of "Mother" fame, spent a great deal of time pre-envisioning his paintings in such detail, that when he mentally "saw" the completed work, he blended his paints into their ultimate hues on his palette. Applying the colors to the canvas was swiftly done.

Other artists begin with a hazier image from which they draw one or more preliminary sketches. They follow with layers of paint—brushstroke by brushstroke, a day's work often scraped off and begun again—then change and add to the original idea until they get as close as they can to what they now know they want.

The same spectrum of methods applies to writing a novel, even one as crafted as a mystery.

Plotting, our pre-envisioning, creates a road map for the trip ahead. You can either plan your entire route in advance or proceed knowing only a general direction. Either way, you'll get there.

Some people are Whistlers who prepare outlines that can be hundreds of pages long—and are actually first drafts. Others begin with a scrap, and off they go. Their first drafts are exploratory and ultimately become long outlines.

Some writers can pre-envision to a point, and then the only way through the murk ahead is by living the story, i.e., writing it and finding a way through. Elizabeth George's intricately plotted novels are preplanned only to about fifty pages of the manuscript. Then she writes and discovers what else is ahead. But before that, she devotes a great deal of preparation time to the characters, and in so doing, sees possibilities in how they might behave.

Still other writers like Janet LaPierre get as far as they can go on their initial idea, and then they compose a midpoint outline, a look back at what has happened so far. Janet then projects what still has to happen.

Shelley Singer starts her books wherever she has an idea for a scene and continues in every which way and direction until she figures out what connects those scenes.

Michael Connelly knows what the case is going to be and who did it, but from then on, he "wings" it. "I find it's actually the best way to create," he says. "It gives you the most freedom, and you enjoy it the most."

Tony Hillerman "gropes" through, able to see "the details that make a plot come to life" only while, in the mind of the viewpoint character, writing the scene. But he needs to be familiar with the location of the story and the nature of the crime and have a theme plus some idea of one or two characters in addition to the sleuth. P.D. James spends more than a year planning each book she writes. James Lee Burke doesn't know what's happening beyond a scene or two.

Lia Matera, author of twelve mystery and suspense novels, says:

> If, going in, I know too much of what's going to happen, I lose interest. I need to be in suspense as much as the reader does. . . . As you might imagine, this means a tremendous amount of rewriting. Once I figure everything out . . . many scenes no longer work, my clues aren't in place, the moods and tone are likely to be wrong. It would be far less work to outline, and it would certainly mean less hand-wringing and breast-beating. But I would lose my juice for the story, so I guess I'm stuck. . . . I have to be trapped in a corner, unable to write one more word, before I'll continue the painful process of plotting. I'd like to be an outliner, but I resent them for being so smug about something that's probably genetic.

Once finished, now knowing where the story has taken him, Tony Hillerman rewrites the first or first few chapters. He says, "You don't have to be able to outline a plot if you have a reasonably long life expectancy."

Beneath all the spins you'll put on it, your basic story is either how the protagonist/sleuth finds or vanquishes the villain or how the proposed victim and/or sleuth prevents the ultimate disaster from happening. So somewhere near the beginning you have to present the problem.

## LET YOUR MIND WANDER AROUND POSSIBILITIES

For example's sake, say you're intrigued by a news story about an embezzler. You were awed by his cleverness, appalled by his chutzpa or terrified that somebody in your office is doing the same thing. Doesn't matter. You were emotionally affected. You decided to use his crime as the basis of your mystery.

Where could a murder (for your mystery's sake) fit into this embezzling scenario? Why? How? Who?

Begin with who was killed and why. This why, the motive, leads you into the back story (What happened leading up to the murder? What is the reason for it?), which is much of what your sleuth is going to have to uncover.

Now, who? The corpse might be the embezzler, the embezzler's boss, the mailroom clerk who happened upon an incriminating bit of evidence, or somebody who was there to deliver a warrant or flowers.

Or maybe there's no dead body—yet. There need not be one immediately, just a sense of impending danger. But the crime should happen relatively early in the book, since it generates much of the action. If you're aiming for suspense—the bad thing that's going to happen—you may think about the crime in a different way. Maybe the embezzler is actually the hapless pawn of someone using his cleverness to destroy the company or wreak revenge on someone. Maybe the embezzler has become our protagonist—trying to break free, go straight, come clean before he's killed, but the noose keeps tightening.

The contemporary puzzle mystery has by and large adopted the traditional suspense finale and no longer pretends that all the suspects would passively gather in the library to be told which of them committed the crime. The contemporary climactic end scene will be a direct, generally physical confrontation with the villain.

## MAKE YOUR WAY THROUGH THE MIDDLE

Now, to figure out how to get from A to Z—what happens in between the crime and the confrontation with the killer. Alas, that space looms as wide as the Grand Canyon, and worse, you've got to build a bridge across it. Nobody ever said it was easy, just possible. It's also possible that the original spelling of *plotting* was *plodding*.

What to do? Consider that crime novels are actually three stories: first, what physically happened; second, the theory of what happened; and third, what really happened. In this case, a dead person in the conference room had a bullet wound. The police decide that poor X was the victim of an interrupted robbery. The actual story is what your sleuth will glimpse in bits and pieces—aka clues—that shine through the surface veil, those facts that don't neatly dovetail with what supposedly happened.

## CREATE SUSPECTS AND ALTERNATE MOTIVES

So that your detective has a serious job ahead of him, think of four other people who, for different reasons, would also appreciate the victim's demise. (His ex-wife who's fatally ill and has come to realize how much money was hidden from her during the divorce. A corrupt cop who was providing security in his off-hours and also, it appears, a bit of special aid and comfort to the dead man's current wife. A woman who, with good cause, sued him for sexual harassment—and lost. A man hired to ghostwrite the victim's autobiography who gets next to nothing—unless the book's a best-seller, which it might be if its subject died violently.)

Write down these reasons and draw lines to the dead person, connecting them. You've got five suspects now, counting the one you know is guilty. Five ways the crime might have happened. You've also got five aspects of the dead man's life, paths for your sleuth to follow into blind alleys and finally, home. Write bios of those people explaining who they are, why they hated the dead person, why they don't have a clear alibi or behave oddly when informed of the news or questioned by the sleuth. Think about what else in their life they're protecting or hiding that will make them suspicious. I like to have every suspect lie. Most are hiding minor embarrassments; some, real but unrelated offenses. But they all twist the truth to serve their own purposes, and that makes the sleuth's job harder by generating wrong theories and misdirection.

## WHAT DOESN'T FIT ABOUT THIS CASE?

Why isn't this an open-and-shut case? If it seems to be one, why does your sleuth disagree with that opinion? What's odd about the murder to the sleuth? What is the initial—and erroneous—theory of what happened and why? Why does the sleuth think this isn't right?

## HOW WOULD YOUR AMATEUR SLEUTH BECOME INVOLVED IN THIS CASE?

If you aren't writing a police procedural, how does your sleuth come to be involved in this crime, and why aren't the police functioning adequately? (This is when you'll envy those who are writing historical mysteries set in the days before there were official police forces.) This is often where what Alfred Hitchcock called the "MacGuffin" comes in. This is an element that gets the story going, often a gimmick that seems to be the issue—missing papers, a Maltese falcon—but isn't the actual problem that will drive the mystery. A MacGuffin, a side or secondary issue, may pull your amateur sleuth—or PI who isn't allowed to investigate an open homicide—into action. Or it may set the police off in the wrong direction, but all the same, pull them into the actual story. If you use a MacGuffin, be sure its question is also answered, ideally before we get to the solution of the real question.

Is there a way to link the crime to the amateur's job? By virtue of her profession or personal life, does your sleuth know something seemingly unrelated to the crime and only she sees the connection?

Sometimes the amateur is driven to action because she's the prime suspect, but obviously, this can't be used too often if you're planning a series. Which of the suspects might she know or have access to so as to sleuth in some sane fashion? Did something she did or said make it worse for her buddy so that she feels obliged to do penance via sleuthing? Does she work for the embezzler? Date the biographer? Have her hair done at the same salon as the ex-wife?

She might be linked to a bit player who'll provide one significant piece of the puzzle or a lead toward it—witnesses, friends of friends, informants, gossips who unwittingly know something valuable, e.g., the dead man's fiancée or cleaning woman. ("And Lord knows what a mess his closet was with that shredder in there. No wonder he kept it locked—must have been ashamed of its looking like a big packing crate in there. Had to beg him to let me clean the place out every three months, and he took off from work so he could stand there watching me the whole time. Peculiar man, rest his soul.")

49

## HOW IS YOUR SLEUTH LINKED TO OTHER CHARACTERS?

Figure out how your detective will reach some of the players. Could she be a client of the same cleaning woman as the now dead embezzler? If so, set it up early. Coincidence is fine to start events rolling but never to solve the crime. So before you need the connection, establish that the cleaning lady exists—she's late, she's switching days with another client—something to make her later appearance feel natural. Are there links to any of the other suspects that need a preliminary establishing scene or mention? Everything in your book that will eventually provide a surprise needs to be set up so the reader feels you played fair. Even if he's forgotten what you set up by the time it resurfaces, he'll then remember that you did establish that fact.

If you have a PI and local law says PIs cannot investigate open homicide cases, then what permissible work is he doing that leads into this murder? Often his assigned case is something of a MacGuffin— not the real problem at all—but his involvement in it pulls him into something darker and more dangerous.

If it's a police case, what makes it more than a run-of-the-mill case, of personal meaning to the detective?

## WHAT HAS TO HAPPEN BEFORE THE REST CAN HAPPEN?

Next, ask yourself what has to happen in order to set up the crime and its discovery. Can you begin with the sleuth walking in on the dead man in the conference room, or are there things we need to know beforehand? Sometimes, you need to plant clues before the crime is committed—action or dialogue by the impending victim, something the sleuth doesn't particularly notice at the time, but in context, will later recall. You might need to set up where your sleuth is before and during the crime so that his arrival at the inauspicious time and his weak alibi make sense.

You want to introduce all your significant characters fairly early in the book, so think of ways to bring them onstage. This may be obvious, but it's worth saying: You *never* want to spring the hitherto unseen villain on the reader at the end.

Let your mind float. See what follows what-ifs. Ask questions: How did this happen? Why would she be there? What would she do if she were there? Free-associate. Don't strain to organize at this point.

You can make anything happen if you make us believe this person would do that. Think about the character and why he'd behave a certain way. As always, check your reflex actions. If your first thought is that your character would run away from the situation, take a moment to consider whether a different course of action might be equally plausible but less predictable and more interesting.

## BUILD THE PLOT WITH FALSE LEADS

What makes certain people suspects? Where were they at the time of the crime? Your sleuth will track down these false leads. You can arrange these discoveries and scenes beginning with the least revealing and most confusing in order to keep the puzzle spinning.

For example: Ethel, the sexual harassment plaintiff, now works in another town. In order to time the killing so precisely, she had to know the details of the victim's erratic schedule. How did she know? How'd she get into the office before it was open? How did Ethel, who does not drive and has only one leg, get to the scene of the crime? How will your sleuth find these things out in order to formulate a theory?

A chapter might be built around discovering that Ethel was not where she should be at the time of the crime; Ethel had hired an airport limo that morning. (How'd the sleuth find that out? Picking through Ethel's trash—another scene? Wait, what made the sleuth do that? However you set it up, we find out that Ethel went to the airport that morning at dawn.) We've reached a seeming dead end—Ethel was in the air when the murder happened. Perhaps the sleuth takes a new tack, looks with more interest at somebody else.

Then, elsewhere, another scene is built around the discovery that Ethel wasn't carrying luggage when she got into that limo and she immediately took a second shuttle from the airport to downtown, one block from the scene of the crime. Motive and opportunity. The sleuth revises the theory again, starts tracking Ethel, but guess what? Just as she's about to be declared the murderer, Ethel is found dead. The logic of the puzzle changes one more time and becomes more urgent; it's now obvious that the killer is willing to kill again rather than be caught.

Maybe. Or maybe Ethel's death had nothing to do with the other crime. When that's realized, the theory will again need revision.

Eventually, you'll have a list of things that have to happen, each of which will become a scene that provides either a real or imagined clue or frustration as the sleuth hits another brick wall. Each plot point changes the status quo, and as in physics, each action produces a reaction—something else now needs to be figured out or done.

## AVOID PLOT CLICHÉS

Throughout, remember that character is destiny and your character is not an idiot. You want drama, but not because of behavior that makes the reader want to shake your sleuth silly. Avoid such plot machinations as having your protagonist agree to meet a suspect on a lonely pier late at night.

Resist plot clichés such as:
- the scene where someone tells the sleuth that they possess vital information they'll share—later. Of course, that someone will be dead before a word of it is uttered.
- the idiotic police force or DA. Make the officials' inability to solve this crime based on inadequate methodology or incorrect assumptions, but not plot-convenient denseness or orneriness.
- the villain who postpones killing the protagonist because he needs to brag about how clever he's been. He hasn't been clever enough to read mysteries and see that during his monologue, our hero's going to figure a way out of this.

If you've read and seen something too often for it ever to feel new again, don't waste your time trying to write it.

Tell yourself your story often. You'll probably see more details each time. At each juncture ask, "What's the worst thing that could happen here?" and go for it. You'll increase the tension and advance the plot.

## SUBPLOTS

You may have been told you need subplots, and indeed, they can enrich your story. But rather than thinking of them as extras plots you need to create, simply consider what else is going on in the protagonist's life beside foiling an evildoer. Is he also facing a love, health, family, professional or financial impasse? How might that impact, reflect, enrich or further complicate the main story? What about the other characters? Remember, your story is what happens at the intersection of many people's individual stories. These other issues will come out of your characters and enrich the mix. Resolve these minor, secondary issues before you resolve the main one: the villain's guilt and apprehension.

## ORGANIZE YOUR IDEAS

Transfer your jumble of doodles, lines, names and ideas to a more manageable medium. Screenwriters use index cards, putting one scene—one thing that has to happen—on each card. Phrase your sentences as actions: "She visits the limo company, but they refuse to open their records." If you can, also note the purpose of the scene: "She's so mad now. She's not worrying about protecting Ethel anymore, and she decides to go to the police." Such cues will generate action and remind you of motive and cause and effect more than, say, "checks out limo company."

Try to put characters into as many of your scenes as possible so you don't always have your solitary sleuth ruminating. Interaction with others is dramatic and provides tension: The sleuth wants information, and the person being interviewed doesn't want to or can't provide it. Dialogue is action.

Eventually you'll have a tableful of cards that will reveal where holes are. Don't worry if it seems scrappy; it's good, and necessary, to leave room for surprises. But the cards might show that you have your sleuth in two places at once or arriving at a conclusion that has nothing supporting it. Or you might see that nothing much happens for a long spell. That plot problem was supposedly solved by Raymond Chandler by bringing in "a man with a gun." It's not a bad plan. Create action. Up the tension by introducing a new threat; always think in terms of "what's the worst that could happen now?" or some dramatic change of your characters' behavior.

Play with the order of scenes: Take one away, combine the points of two of them into one solid scene, and so forth. If you hit a wall now—or in the writing process—when your character seemingly has become paralyzed and can't function usefully, look back and see if you can change the given that's halted present action. Does your sleuth really, truly have to be a Siamese twin?

## THE THREE-ACT STRUCTURE

It can be useful to think in terms of stage and screen. Your drama, too, will have three acts. Your first act is roughly the first third of the book. Here you set up and present the crime, establishing the conflict. You also introduce your cast of characters, their relationships and your setting.

The second act, usually the bulk of the book, is devoted to complications and crises: the great middle muddle—the sleuthing in a mystery, further threats and escalating dangers in suspense. Protagonists try and fail and try again.

In fact, there is almost a "rule of three." The initial attempt establishes the problem and its difficulty, and nobody succeeds. If they did, there'd be no story. The second attempt and failure show that it's a really big problem and not at all easily solved, and the third becomes the real test that breaks the pattern. (A fourth try seems excessive—give your sleuth a break!) This is true in almost all quest stories and fairy tales. It's a pattern that works.

So theories prove wrong, often by the introduction of a second corpse—most often, the former prime suspect—and we try again. The tension is now sky high.

The third act eliminates more theories, thereby tying up subplots while building to "The Big Scene"—that do-or-die point of no return, the crisis when the sleuth finally figures it out and confronts the villain or the suspense protagonist finally meets his demon face-to-face.

End with a brief coda for closure. This isn't an explanation of what you've already shown, but a page or two giving the reader an idea of what's ahead or what the events meant to the protagonist.

## IF THAT OUTLINE DOESN'T WORK . . .

When you write the first draft, no matter how much time and effort you lavished on your outline, parts of it will probably not work. New ideas will occur to you as you live the story, and you'll be wise to go with them and say adios to your original plans.

The outline is a road map. The writing is the trip—and the real adventure.

# 9 WHAT YOU DON'T KNOW...

Your readers are part of this adventure. They're pitting themselves against your sleuth even though they want to be outsmarted by him. But the challenge dissipates if the reader realizes he knows more than either your protagonist or you. People who will suspend disbelief in amazing ways will complain if you mess up your facts. Some readers will close a book on page 1 if they discover a glaring error in how a wet suit works or which way a street runs.

This is partly because one of the enjoyable side benefits of your book is effortless learning. The reader wants to believe that if you say a gun sounds a certain way, it does. Your plot can be as far-fetched and credulity stretching as you want to make it, but your revolver can't be silent just because you've seen too many movies where silencers muted all sound. According to my research, a sound suppressor can't go on a revolver, and even if it could, the revolver still makes noise. You want to know such things so that your reader doesn't pull back and out of your spell.

But given that we're not omniscient, what's a writer to do? How do we write what we *don't* know? We do research. Let your imagination fly into the stratosphere—but stay grounded with the facts. In this information-rich world, you can find out pretty much anything you need to know. And you'd better.

## INTERVIEWS

Let's begin with an excellent, low-tech information source: people who know things. Interviews are invaluable chances to gather data along with a sense of how it's presented, the jargon of a trade. In person, you can pick the significant details, the ones that make this story uniquely yours. Interviews can also produce plot ideas or embellishments. Two of my favorite questions are what most bothers a person about his work and whether anything odd has happened lately at work. Both have revealed aspects I'd never considered, and those led to twists in plots and, I hope, added further depth to my story.

We're all eager to share our special expertise, so people are generally quite willing to talk with you. If they have time, take them out for lunch or a drink. In either case, thank them afterwards, acknowledge them in your novel and give them a copy of the published book.

Don't hold your interview in a state of total ignorance. First, find out what you can about the topic by reading about it. Think about it and your plans for your novel and what you need to know. Save your questions—and your interviewee's time—for those aspects that aren't easily researched elsewhere. Saying "tell me everything about neurosurgery (or your training as a pilot or life in Hawaii)" is going to yield a stunned silence. Prepare yourself.

Even if you're looking for an exotic, remote, unusual occupation, given the six-degrees-of-separation theory, you can usually find someone who knows someone who knows . . . whatever you want to know—or how to find out about it.

If you're looking for the wrong or illegal way to do something, check with experts on how to do it correctly or legally. The security company can help you understand how a system (not theirs, of course) could be circumvented. The locksmith knows how people pick locks. The fire department knows about arson and how to detect it. Your neighborhood mechanic will have ideas on how to tamper with a car and make it dangerous.

## PUBLIC INFORMATION OFFICERS AND
## OTHER POLICE SOURCES

Unless you're writing a historical novel set in the eras before professional crime fighters, do your homework about law enforcement. Even the amateur sleuth works against a backdrop of professionals, so do your own sleuthing. This applies to all governmental bureaus: the FBI; Immigration; Alcohol, Tobacco and Firearms; and state troopers. Don't guess how they work or rely on other writers' guesses. Contact their public relations person. Explain that you're a freelance writer and want to get your facts right, and they'll be pleased to help.

Most urban police forces have information officers whose job is to help the public understand police work. Explain what you're doing and ask away. You can continue the six-degrees-of-separation chain by asking your new sources in law enforcement how you can keep up with the latest in forensic science. Today's plots have to acknowledge the existence of DNA testing and other formerly unknown technologies.

Some police departments have citizen "ride along" programs or civilian police academies for much the same purpose as the public information office. This could be invaluable for a sense of what the police do, as well as what they know about the realities of the area. It's also worthwhile to listen to the voices of authentic members of a given profession, including the police. Their idiosyncratic but authentic stories, their often black sense of humor, the jargon they use and the assumptions they make can enrich your writing.

Consider taking an administration of justice course, generally offered through community colleges. Extension and learning centers often have courses called "Become a PI!" and while you might not be ready to put on gumshoes, both the instructor and the course material can help make your PI more believable.

## TOURS, COURSES, CONFERENCES AND BOOKS

The local morgue or coroner's office can help with issues of procedure. Some big-city morgues actually have guided tours.

Universities in your area might have courses on forensic specialties taught by experts in various disciplines. See if they can help you— even if it's by directing you elsewhere or giving you a reading list.

Look for specialized conferences. The mystery world is full of them, in all parts of the country. Some are geared toward readers, some toward writers, some to both, and they might include panel discussions by and access to crime professionals. There are also forensic conferences that might admit a nonpro.

A variety of helpful books exist. The Howdunit writing series published by Writer's Digest Books has volumes detailing poisons, crime scene investigation, weapons, missing persons, con games and more. Scientific presses produce books on forensics designed for professionals. They aren't for the faint of heart, but they are full of potential plots. Michael Connelly has said that he found the seed of *The Concrete Blonde* by reading one such book's description of an actual case.

A visit to your local courthouse to watch a trial will teach you about the realities of the court system. If a lawyer considers an interview a billable hour, contact law professors for help with legal issues.

## VISIT SITES IN PERSON OR "VIRTUALLY"

Your setting also has to be grounded. I live outside San Francisco, and, along with all Bay Area denizens, I am vastly annoyed when I see a film that has everybody crossing the Golden Gate Bridge, no matter where they're headed. And just about every film does.

Annoyance is bad. It pulls me out of the movie's world, just as it would pull your reader out of yours. The best way to make sure your facts are correct is to check them firsthand, to visit your sites, even if you lived or live nearby or are certain you know them. I find it useful to carry a camera and small tape recorder. I get more details down by dictating them than by trying to write notes. When I'm meandering along with the recorder, I mention noises, smells, nearby traffic and anything else that might be relevant. And I take a lot of photos.

But don't despair if you can't visit your setting. Writers of historical mysteries can't visit theirs, so do what they do—research. Investigate the wealth of material provided by chambers of commerce, tourist information bureaus, local historical societies, travel books and videos, local newspapers (generally available in libraries, large newsstands, by direct subscription or on-line), local magazines, street maps and unique books about a place—guides to its architecture or botany. Your librarian can help track such titles for potential interlibrary loans.

A research librarian can also help you gain access to special collections, so you can find out whether early cars had windshield wipers or what an elegant dinner would have cost in New York City in 1925.

Oral histories are wonderful for the details that standard histories omit, such as folk remedies, how holidays were celebrated and how courtships were arranged. Many historical societies have gathered and printed collections of these.

Don't forget local experts. With a little patience, six degrees of separation works here as well. Somebody's cousin's best friend's uncle is out there, waiting to tell you what you need to know. Ask around.

Libraries have catalogs, newspapers and magazines from the past, and they're valuable for small details—not only the articles, but the ads, the prices, the fads that died out, issues since resolved that we might otherwise forget were once red hot. Specialized libraries have industry publications—trade and in-house magazines—that add texture, with their details of different jobs and advice and warnings to people in the industry.

Professional researchers, who, for a fee, will search for whatever it is you need to know, are listed in the phone book.

## THE WEB
There is, of course, the immense potential of the ever expanding World Wide Web. The Internet will have much of the above, in one form or another, plus the potential of exchanging E-mail or "talking" on-line with someone in the geographical area or having the special expertise that interests you. The potential of the Internet is enormous—as long as you eventually tear yourself away from it and use the computer to write your book.

## SISTERS IN CRIME
Sisters in Crime is an international organization (with members of the sisterly *and* brotherly persuasions) of published crime writers, people who hope to publish and people who simply enjoy reading mysteries. Over the years, they've evolved into many overlapping subgroups and are extremely helpful with all the issues that plague crime writers. You can reach them by mail: Executive Secretary, Sisters in Crime, P.O. Box 442124, Lawrence, KS 66044-8933.

## "VET" YOUR MANUSCRIPT
If you've made friends with your sources along the way, perhaps you can get them to "vet" the manuscript once it's done—if not the entire manuscript, then the pages on which you're using their profession. You aren't asking for literary criticism, just whether the character sounds right. Would a real pathologist talk that way? Do those things?

## AFTER ALL THAT, DON'T LET YOUR RESEARCH SHOW
You want to put us into a world—not into a museum tour. So find out what your characters need to know and make it work for the story. If it doesn't—if it's too obviously there because, by gum, you worked hard to get to know it and you're going to tell the world—it will produce a book that will seem as clumsy as a ballerina grunting with exertion.

Put the portions that don't work into that file with your redundant characters and think about another book or story that might give them active, meaningful roles.

Researching is *your* chance to sleuth. Enjoy it.

# 10 MAKING THE READER CARE

A mystery is, above all, a story. And though our stories involve crimes and villains, we nonetheless want our readers to identify with our characters and to feel emotions of horror, confusion, elation, fear, relief, excitement—*something*. In fact, our readers demand it.

Nonfiction may also want to make you feel an emotion. An article may aim at rousing the public against elder abuse, but it will do so through a reasoned explanation of conditions. It will use data and facts.

Mystery writers instead *dramatize* the situation. Our victim might be an elderly person in a helpless and increasingly horrifying and ultimately fatal situation. Instead of being told how dreadful life is for people caught in this abuse, by identifying with the character and her struggles, the reader would himself experience the problem.

Fiction tries to reproduce the emotional impact of experience. We don't want you to read all about it. We want you to *live* it, to reach understanding via gut-level reactions rather than through an appeal to your mind. This is not to say mystery fiction can't be full of ideas, but those ideas will be conveyed more effectively if you make your reader walk in someone else's shoes.

This is basic human psychology. If you tell me conditions are bad for many elderly people, I'll reflexively adopt an "Oh, yeah? Says who? Prove it" reaction. But if what I experienced—through a character—made me reach the same conclusion, I'll believe it. We trust first-hand experience. Fiction gives that to its readers.

If readers aren't emotionally moved by the actions of the characters, they won't care what's happening, no matter how significant the theme, how clever the concept or how many car chases, violent deaths and semiviolent matings are part of the action. We want to care, we want to feel, we want to be personally involved—to *be* the characters, live their lives, feel their emotions.

Suppose while you were watching the Winter Olympics, the screen went blank and the announcer said, "Wow! I've never seen anything that wonderful! Incredible—a quadruple spin and flip—the move of the century, folks. Wasn't that exciting?" Wouldn't you feel cheated? You wanted to experience that yourself, and if you had, you'd have felt the excitement, too.

Your reader doesn't want you telling him "Wow! That fellow is really bad—evil and sneaky." He wants to see it himself.

## SHOW, DON'T TELL

The mystery writer's primary obligation is to dramatize events and let them reveal their own meanings, not to stand on the sidelines and preach, telling readers how to feel about people or events. We present evidence, not judgments.

We do that on paper precisely as we do it in life. All human experience is apprehended through our sensory apparatus. In plain English: We find out about the world by seeing, feeling, hearing, tasting and smelling. Then we process those impressions and reach judgments— "lovely voice," "handsome man," "rotten idea," "pompous fool," "uh-oh, something's wrong here."

Nobody goes outside and *feels* "another rotten winter morning." Instead, we go outside and our cheeks sting, eyes water, sinuses ache and toes smart. We notice that the wind howls, cars skid, light dims, tree limbs twist, heavy clouds press the horizon. We may smell snow or rain in the air. And then we conclude, through the details we've accumulated, that what we have here is indeed "another rotten winter morning." The convincing proof was the sensory data. You, the author, must put in that proof in order to make your case.

The next time something in print makes you laugh or cry or hold your breath in anxious anticipation, check the writing and see if it wasn't specific sensory details that got to you, i.e., made you live through and therefore comprehend the experience.

If your character is meant to be arrogant, bland, compassionate, pompous, nervous, bigoted, stingy, ambitious, you have to find sensory details that show the reader what you mean.

## Specific details, not abstractions

An abstraction names a quality, characteristic or idea. It does not convey data to the senses. Our favorite catchwords—such as "beauty," "love," "all-American," "patriotic"—are abstract. These are intellectual concepts, demanding thought rather than emotion. They are also ambiguous, subject to endless interpretation and redefinition. "She's beautiful," your mother says of the blind date she arranged for you, and that is when you realize how differently two people can define the same word. Instead of an abstraction, you needed specific details in order to get the picture.

The very vagueness of abstractions that works for politicians ("Hey, he's for patriotism and so am I. I'll vote for him!") works against writers of fiction, because we paint our pictures. It is not our reader's job to provide the images. We promised to make him feel something by putting him in the world we've created. We can't do that with amorphous intellectual constructs.

The unfortunate truth is that it's much easier to write abstract telling words (and to feel terribly literary in the doing) than to reproduce—through vivid, definite details—what the characters actually saw or felt. But since the strength of good prose is based on concrete, specific language, it's worth the extra effort.

Here's an example of telling via abstractions:

> I lay on a bed in a seedy hotel where none of the furnishings were good. The bed was hard and uncomfortable and the mattress thin. It was in a noisy, congested neighborhood with a lot of car and foot traffic outside.

Is that writer's "seedy" my "seedy"? Is his definition of an uncomfortable mattress mine? Am I seeing something even close to the room he envisioned?

But what about:

> I lay on my back on a bed in a waterfront hotel and waited for it to get dark. It was a small front room with a hard bed and a mattress slightly thicker than the cotton blanket that

covered it. A spring underneath me was broken and stuck into the left side of my back. I lay there and let it prod me.

The reflection of a red neon light glared on the ceiling. When it made the whole room red it would be dark enough to go out. Outside cars honked along the alley they called the Speedway. Feet slithered on the sidewalks below my window. There was a murmur and mutter of coming and going in the air. The air that seeped in through the rusted screens smelled of stale frying fat. Far off a voice of the kind that could be heard far off was shouting: "Get hungry, folks. Get hungry. Nice hot doggies here. Get hungry."

—Raymond Chandler, *Farewell, My Lovely*

Look at the sensory data in that passage: the broken spring in his back, the light on the ceiling telling time as it changes, the smells, the murmurs and mutters audible to us as well. Then *we* decide this is a seedy hotel. Chandler painted a picture with a few specific details and invited us in. He didn't tell us what to think of it.

Consider the emotions you want your images to provoke, and choose your details carefully. To be specific, *be specific*. Put a sign above your desk that says "see-feel-hear-smell-touch."

### Create a sensory data bank

Become aware of the sensory input of your life and collect impressions that have emotional overtones for you. We don't have a great vocabulary for textures, smells or tastes, so you may want to think of comparisons. Hair like . . . the odor of. . . . But don't forget the power of existing words, particularly verbs that convey sensory data. We can hear the object's sound through *lisp, boom, splash, shrill, whir*. We can feel the substance through *slick, greasy, gritty, steaming, nubby, furry, hairy, ice-cold*. We can taste the substance through *creamy, peppery, tart, mellow, sour, sugary, salty, bitter*. We can smell the environment through *rancid, musk, incense, lemony, ammonia, stench*. Don't think about style or being literary. Instead, be honest.

### Find the detail that conveys emotion

The selection of those specific sensory details that enable your reader to live your vision isn't a random process. You're looking for the trait

63

that reveals something of significance. Rather logically, we call this the *significant detail*.

You'll pick which details to use depending on what effect you want to create, and then you'll discreetly leave. The reader, your partner in crime, will complete the picture with his own experience and vision and make the story his own.

## WRITE WHAT YOU KNOW?

"Write what you know" is second only to "Show, don't tell" in the basic annals of writing wisdom. However, this should not be taken literally—particularly by mystery writers. Think of the chaos and bloodshed we'd wreak if we truly had to write only what we knew. And when would we find the time to write?

As I said, do your research. But understand that you already know the most important thing a writer needs to know. You know what it's like to be a human being, and that, no matter the subject, is what you'll write about.

Flaubert said "Madame Bovary, *c'est moi*." He wasn't an adulterous housewife, and you aren't a killer—but you can identify with your characters because we're all made of the same basic ingredients. Some people have more of one part, a paucity of another, but that's a matter of degree, not substance. Everybody's felt at least a twinge of every human emotion by now (even a stifled, but fleeing urge towards homicide). Push the bit you've felt to extremes when needed; make the character obsessed by it if need be. We all have the same emotions of pain, loss, fear and rage, and only what triggers them and how they are expressed makes them pathological. And that is why you, the writer, can become anyone and make the reader believe in the portrait you're painting.

If you want to write about a homicidal maniac, you can, even if you aren't (yet?) one. Or if you've been a Sherpa guide all your life and now you want to write about a timid data processor who accidentally becomes involved in a serious crime, you can. Or suppose you're an outdoorsman fascinated by what might happen if a woman with debilitating environmental allergies were harassed out of her apartment. . . .

The doors are wide open. Go ahead. You may need to research homicidal patterns, data processing and office workers, or environmental allergies, but you already know the human basics. And your human readers will love seeing the truth of that on the page.

# 11 STRUCTURING YOUR MYSTERY

Now you know something about your story material. You have building blocks—a group, large or small, of plot elements, and characters who will experience the events—but where do you put what you have so as to build a mystery out of them? Where and how do you begin and end? How do you make it exciting and mysterious and include all the information you need? What about transitions?

We're now looking at the structure of your novel. It may help to think of your book as a living organism with a spine that is your basic idea: X shot and killed Y in the office conference room because. . . . Each scene you attach to it is a muscle that fleshes out and helps move the beast. The important word here is *attach* because scenes will in some way connect to your premise. If not, they're flab weighing down your creature. Of course, some material may need to be there to set up something else that is directly relevant to the sleuth's efforts.

## TWO WAYS TO PRESENT MATERIAL

You can *summarize* chunks of time and tell us what happened during them. For example: "The seasons passed quickly, one after the other," or "For months she stayed in her room, unable to face them."

Or you can *dramatize* important chunks of time and show us what happened in a *scene* so we hear it, see it, experience it firsthand. "Show, don't tell" plays here, too.

### Scenes and when to use them

Scenes are essential to fiction. Scenes have in miniature everything your novel has—conflict, characters, a crisis and a change. The situation is not exactly the same at the end as it was at the beginning. Important moments for your story cannot be taken offstage and summarized. If you think about it, this imitates human psychology.

When little of emotional significance happens in our lives, we say, "Nothing happened." This can apply to a few moments or entire years of which we have only a vague sense. Of course things happened— we worked, dreamed, socialized, aged—but *something* is reserved for emotion-packed moments that are vividly remembered, often with complete sensory recollection. We recall what we wore, what she said, the perfume someone had on, background music. We recall scenes.

Imitate reality. If it's a turning point, a vital moment, make it a scene. If it's a time when nothing particularly relevant to your story happened, summarize it.

The flip side of this is that if you do dramatize something, the reader will assume it's important—that the premise and outcome are somehow affected by it—so make sure it is.

To avoid monotony, vary the length of scenes and the number of characters in them. It's awfully easy to fall into the trap of having your sleuth slog from person to person, asking questions, getting answers and moving on.

### Transitions between scenes

So you are varying your scenes—now how do you move us from one to the other?

The easiest way is via that familiar double space followed by a sentence establishing where the new scene has placed us and in whose sensibilities. If the in-between events are irrelevant, we've avoided dawdling. The reader automatically understands that a double space means a break of some sort—that we're shifting to another point of view, another place or another time.

You can also summarize. Very often, a chapter is basically a scene. One unit of thought or action. One step in the ongoing story. One clue achieved. You can end this scene at a high point, then begin the next chapter/scene with a brief summary, e.g., "Three days later, she received a phone call. . . ."

### The order of scenes

The King of Hearts's advice on telling stories during Alice's adventures is still good: "Begin at the beginning, and go on till you come to the end: then stop." This is the best, easiest and least intrusive way. Start with a problem and end with its solution.

This means the beginning of this story. Not the sleuth's beginnings—his humble birth, his rise to fame—but this story that answers the question you're raising.

We're dealing with crime, so the beginning of this dramatic change could translate into an opening line of "Harry lay dead on the floor." But you run a risk with a grabber of this sort. Harry is no more than a name to us at this point, and the rest of the people who might be involved or concerned aren't even names yet. There's no reason for us to care why Harry's there. Given that risk, and in order to show us the meaning of the change in Harry's fortunes, it's probably necessary to set the scene, to give the reader a sense of how things were before everything changed. Begin just before the character is presented with a dilemma or the first hints that a major problem looms. (These hints are called *foreshadowing*—a promise that conflict lies ahead if the reader just stays tuned.)

The idea is to begin your novel as close as possible to the actions that shape it. In a mystery, this means as close as possible to the crime that triggers the story of detection. The literary term for this place to start is *in medias res*, "in the middle of things." Necessary scene-setting is part of the "as close as possible."

Give only what is necessary for us to know right then as background. Remember that you have about three hundred manuscript pages in which to fill in more about your people and situation—about what really happened and why. Even knowing this, we all write too much at the beginning, so don't worry about that right now. You'll be writing what you need to know. It's possible that later on, you'll see that the reader doesn't need to know all that—at least not right then.

## WHAT THE READER NEEDS TO KNOW RIGHT AWAY

You make an unspoken contract with your reader promising that what's up front is important. He'll pay close attention to what you tell him right away because he believes—even if he's not conscious of it—that this will be relevant. So if you show us that the character carries a gun, its existence had better matter at some point.

Since you're only giving an impression of the character, his setting and situation, pick the relevant details—those significant details. Don't frustrate your reader by making him store too much, most of which he doesn't need at all. He'd rather get into your story.

Up front, we need to know the protagonist's sex, approximate age, general locale and condition (urban, rural, educated, criminal), and we need a hint of the problem—but don't reveal everything. There will be lots of time later, after the action has started rolling.

What you want to do with that opening is give a sense that something worth pursuing awaits the reader if she'll just hang in there. You want to hook her and reel her in by intriguing her with a character, a setting, an action or a combination of these things. Look how Jan Burke uses character to pull us in, and then immediately establishes tension with a surprising second line in *Goodnight, Irene*.

> He loved to watch fat women dance. I guess O'Connor's last night on the planet was a happy one because that night he had an eyeful of the full-figured.

Carolyn Wheat's *Troubled Waters* hooks us with a situation and an attitude that is puzzling and compels us to read on, to find out why:

> I thought she was dead.
>
> I hoped she was dead.
>
> But she was very much alive, too damned much alive, and her thin, nervous face stared at me from the front pages of every newspaper on the Court Street kiosk.
>
> Jan was back. She'd been working at a Wal-Mart in Emporia, Kansas. One day she left work early and drove to Kansas City, where she walked into the FBI office in the federal building and turned herself in.

We don't know what Jan had or hadn't done or why the narrator wished Jan were dead, but because it doesn't compute, because it goes against polite expectations, it intrigues. We'll hang in there to find out what it means.

Joe Gores starts *Contract Null & Void* using foreshadowing with menacing situation, language and setting:

> He was north of the Golden Gate Bridge on the Coast Highway, pumping his way up the steep hairpin turn without even breathing hard. What he carried was fitting for Walpurgis Night, when witches supposedly made rendezvous with the devil—*Allemands à l'excès*, with their fear of

women! Even his light expensive racing bike was a sort of parallel for the broomsticks—or he-goats—the witches rode.

The last of the light was gone, even far out across the Pacific, but he'd ridden this route a hundred times, day, night, in heat, in icy cold, in blinding fog, drizzle, outright rain—it held no terrors for him despite the almost sheer cliff face a few feet from his spinning tires.

Nobody knew where he was; since they'd come looking he'd been a ghost, a wraith, nothing more than a rumor.

Nancy Pickard at the start of *Confession* tells us very little except that something unforgettable—fate itself—haunts her, and with only that powerful foreshadowing, she pulls us in:

I still have fantasies about the day when fate came riding up to our house like "The Highwayman" in the old poem: "*Riding, riding, riding, up to the old inn door . . .*"

Only in this case, on this particular Sunday in that specific August, it wasn't an inn that he came riding up to, and he wasn't a man yet, and I wasn't an innkeeper's black-haired daughter. It was our home, and he was just a boy, and I was a policeman's wife.

Even so, the refrain is inescapable: "*. . . the highwayman came riding . . .*"

In some of my fantasies of that day I get a chance to cheat fate: I get to spy fate as it speeds down the highway toward us as determinedly as a meteor slamming toward earth.

See how in an unconventional, strong, near poetic Southern story-telling voice Margaret Maron in *Up Jumps the Devil* establishes her protagonist, the setting and a hearty dose of tension by letting us know there's been a murder and the protagonist did something mistakenly:

Most of my brothers—

Most of my respectable brothers, that is—

(Which also includes the ones that've sowed all their wild oats and are now settling into gray-haired middle age and trying to pretend they've been respectable all along.)

(When you have eleven older brothers, it's sometimes hard to keep straight which ones have walked the line their

69

whole lives and which ones are newly whitened sepulchers.)

Anyhow, most of my brothers say I don't think long enough before I go rushing off half-cocked.

Usually I'll argue their definition of what's half-cocked, but every once in a while I have to admit that they may have a point.

If I hadn't rushed out to do the right thing when Dallas Stancil got himself shot and killed in his own backyard, I wouldn't have been left looking like a fool.

("Don't bet on it," says Dwight Bryant. He's the deputy sheriff here in Colleton County and might as well be another brother the way he feels free to smart mouth everything I do, even though I'm a district court judge and higher up in the judicial pecking order, technically speaking, than he is.)

These books are all off to a running start, each in its own way. You can feel the story's gears moving under you. But notice that nobody's cramming in every potentially relevant detail. We don't know what color hair O'Connor had; we don't know the name of Gores's bike rider, let alone whether he's married, what his normal occupation is or where he's come from. We know only that a boy came to Pickard's narrator's door. But in all cases, we can wait for more information as it becomes relevant. Right now, all we need is a rough map of the world we're entering—whose is it, where is it, how is it—and a sense that something's going to happen soon.

## WHAT ABOUT BOOKS THAT CAN'T BE STRUCTURED THIS WAY?

In some mysteries, present events are the result of long-buried secrets; others seek to explain how something awful came about—which means they need a long lead-in before the actual event happens. How is suspense maintained in a case like that?

Foreshadowing is one way, as shown above. This is the literary equivalent of the news teaser "dramatic revelations at trial—story at eleven." Basically, you create tension by creating an ominous atmosphere, implying something is going to happen (or has happened, and it's worth waiting for the telling of it) or having your character know or sense that something's amiss or about to happen. And sometimes, simply by establishing—early on—that something's out of kilter, we feel that shadow of trouble ahead. The end of chapter two of *Old Enemies* by Janet LaPierre is an exchange between Meg Halloran and her teenaged daughter, Katy, on a vacation to visit Lauren:

> "What happened to the brother?"
>
> "Who?"
>
> "Lauren's rotten brother."
>
> "Nobody knows. He disappeared about ten years ago."
>
> "He must have been grown up by then," said Katy.
>
> "Just twenty-one, I think. He was extremely handsome, and very wild, and Lauren said he wouldn't work on the ranch and hated living there. She thinks he just ran away, probably because he was in trouble of some kind." As Meg recalled from Lauren's reports at the time, a local girl had turned up soon after Bobby Macrae's disappearance insisting he was the father of her unborn baby. "And he's never bothered to let anyone know where he is."
>
> "Weird," said Katy. "Maybe he'll come home while we're there."
>
> "Oh, Katy, let's hope not."

The reader shivers in anticipation. Of course bad, wild Bobby is going to show up in one form or another, and we're willing to wait as the story builds.

### Don't cheat the reader to build suspense

Do not attempt to raise the tension level by withholding something your point-of-view character knows. ("Suddenly, I understood, felt the whole horror of Joe's situation, read the message in his eyes." [end of chapter]) Like the nasty school-yard taunt of "I know something you don't know," it won't endear you to your reader.

Don't conceal something or cloak it in heavy foreshadowing and dark veiling simply for the sake of mystification. When it turns out to have no significance, your readers will heartily resent you. Foreshadow early, based on tangible facts. The further apart the suggestion of something and the actual thing, the more likely your reader will have forgotten it and be happily surprised by it.

### Frames and prologues

Other ways of structuring a story don't lend themselves to the King of Hearts's "start at the beginning" credo. Often, the author "frames"

71

his story by beginning with a prologue—a scene set earlier or in the present, offstage—then moves directly into the actual story, either leaping ahead in time or going way back to the roots of how that first scene came about and what then happened. Donna Tartt's *The Secret History* begins with the murder of a young man. We know who did it, but we then backtrack to find out why the victim's friends deliberately killed him.

## STARTING AND ENDING SCENES

Starting *in medias res* applies to each scene within the novel, beginning at the moment when what is happening becomes necessary to the action of the story and ending when its point has been made, even though the characters are still talking their heads off. What isn't relevant can be summarized.

Study the next book you enjoy and note how the author skips (or summarizes) the times when nothing much would be said to have happened. Notice how he does the same when the important action of the scene is over. Life is boring; fiction shouldn't be.

In chapters and scenes, end the action when something has changed but not been resolved, thereby introducing suspense that pulls the reader into the next chapter. Look at the following and note that Steven Womack doesn't end this scene in *Dead Folks' Blues* on the peaceful, literally harmonious note that seems the wind-down. Instead, he yanks us back into discordant, confusing urgency:

> The two sang on, their voices blending in a harmony as sweet as clear sunshine. The verses were not sophisticated, but they were genuine and earthy and touching. I felt like I was sitting in on something pretty impressive. Ray and Slim played guitar licks off each other at the end of the song, then note by note, traded off the resolution, hit the final chord, and let the sound echo away into silence inside the office.
>
> Then there was a scream.
>
> [end of chapter]

Think how contented the reader would have been had that last sentence not been there. He'd have been able to close the book and go to sleep. That isn't what you want.

Look how Laurie R. King in *With Child* compels you to turn that page and begin the next chapter:

> There was no pain, no burst of light, no time for fear, much less anger, just the beginning awareness of movement above and behind her, a faint swishing noise registering in her ears, and then Kate was gone. [end chapter six]
>
> [chapter seven] Somewhere, deep down, she was aware. Some part of her concussed and swelling brain smelled the dust on the floor beneath her, heard the boots running toward her and the sirens cutting off, one by one. . . ."

Here King is literally doing what we're all trying to do figuratively— skipping the unconscious time when nothing memorable happened.

## FLASHBACKS

The other potential disruption in the linear telling of a story is the flashback.

A flashback isn't a memory. "Remember when we went skiing in February?" is present action, being said now about something that happened earlier. A flashback is a scene set in the past that tells us something we absolutely must know so that we can understand present action. This is the only justification for its use, since it disrupts the forward motion of your story by pulling the reader out of it, into the past. The urge to find out what happens next is stifled, and if the reader becomes involved in the past action, she feels doubly cheated when you zip her back into present time.

Rather than using flashbacks, show the past through current memory and present conflicts. Refer back briefly, minimally—but not through bad dialogue in which people tell each other what they already know. Use your narrative voice to state the necessary facts, and let the reader proceed.

If you feel you must flash back, try to wait till midbook. You can't enrich a story that hasn't had a chance to get under way. Don't fall for the trap of opening with the bare beginning of a scene—somebody waiting for the door to be answered suddenly remembers everything that led to this moment. If you do use a flashback, follow literary convention and make a sense perception trigger it. The character sees, smells, hears, touches or tastes (remember how the taste of a madeleine cake unlocked several volumes' worth of novelistic memories for

Proust?) something that becomes a powerful emotional link to a past he relives rather than simply remembers.

The technical method for this time travel is as follows:

- If your story is written in past tense ("He borrowed a cigarette from her and immediately recognized its taste"), create a bridge to the past by using the past perfect tense for about two transitional sentences ("It had been late at night, in the cafe. He'd been choking from one too many cigarettes that tasted of camel dung . . ."). Then write the flashback scene in the past tense ("She smacked his back, hard, until . . ."). Segue back into your present story with another one or two transitional sentences in past perfect ("He'd been daydreaming again, he realized, as he stubbed out the cigarette").
- If you're writing in the present tense, follow the same pattern, switching to past tense for the transitions.

Choose whichever tense feels right to you, but keep it consistent.

Make sure the significant action of your story isn't all in the past. If it is, maybe the past *is* your story and you should think about restructuring the entire novel.

End your novel the same way you end your scenes and chapters—while the action and meaning are still interesting. Show us, via ongoing action, as much of your story as you can, and then, having presented the conclusion, don't reflect or summarize. The "Perry Mason afterword," when Della and Perry sat around and explained what we'd seen, is an anticlimax. Perhaps you'll want a page or so to sum up a loose end or present the protagonist's take on the events, but the basic truth is: When you've finished your story, get up and leave.

## PACING

Pacing is built into the structure of your story. We've discussed how a series of conflicts and complications escalates until the do-or-die point when the main conflict is resolved one way or the other. Step-by-step the stakes rise; the problems become more intense and pressing until finally everything hinges on one last chance, and we can barely breathe until we know how this turns out.

If instead of that slow rise to the boil we begin with a slam-bang high point—a terrific grabber—how can we then have rising action for the rest of the book? We drop back, putting in a quieter scene that allows the reader to regain a normal pulse rate. And then we start building up again, albeit more slowly, to other peak moments, until ultimately we're at the climactic scene which is at least a match for the opening one.

Think in terms of hills and valleys, with each peak a little higher. But as action-filled as your peaks may be, leaping from one to the next is boring and will give your story the dramatic depth of a Saturday morning cartoon. The human mind can't handle constant stress. If you bombard it with sound and events it may retreat into catatonia, or at least exhaustion. On the other hand, nobody is suggesting a book-length bicker—a plateau of minor conflict—unless they're looking for a nonprescription sleeping pill. So what to do?

Remember that change is what you're writing about and what readers care about and what provides the sense of forward motion. Build to your big moments. Don't spring them on us. Let your reader share the second-by-second anxiety and growing tension. When something really matters and is emotionally saturated, it happens for us in slow-motion, nightmarish hyper-real time. Play it that way.

Allow for restorative lulls—a calmer scene, a bit of humor (comic relief is well named), a bridge between emotional outbursts. Then clobber them again.

We need to see and understand the changes in both the situation and the character's psychology. If your hero mutates from nervous and withdrawn in one scene to outspoken and assertive about saving the world in the next, we won't believe it. But if you show us he has the potential for this, and then show us the steps that change him, you've got a dramatic and believable scene coming up.

As mentioned in the section on setting, you do *not* have to show every leave-taking, every shift of locale—and you'll bore us to death if you do. But if you do have to show such a relocation, give it emotion and meaning, for example:

> He was shaken to realize he was pulling up to his house. He couldn't remember a single street or building along the way.

It may become obvious later that the summarized ride home is important and should be fully dramatized. On the other hand, something depicted in a scene might prove to have no tension, change or point and should be summarized. Be flexible.

# 12 HOUSEKEEPING AND THE MIDBOOK BLUES

Some ideas to help you stay relatively organized and sane while you're writing your mystery.

## YOUR "BIBLE"

I've mentioned keeping an alphabetical name chart of all your characters and places to avoid giving everyone the same initial. This can be part of a "bible" you keep of place names, characters' names and ages and whatever facts might confuse you later on.

If I mention a specific piece of furnishing in Amanda Pepper's home, I put it in my bible, along with the make of her car, the origins of her school building, how old her sister's children are and the names of co-workers. Also included is anything idiosyncratic, such as likes or dislikes—and in my case, with the Amanda Pepper series, a list of what names she's suggested might fill out C.K.'s initials.

In the course of a series, I also keep notes on when in the character's slow chronology the books were set—what month and season, her age at the time. And I keep a skeleton of the plot—who died and by what method, what the motive was—so that I can avoid unconsciously recycling the same elements, story after story.

## MAKE NOTES, NOT REVISIONS

As you write, try not to stop work to solve questions that arise or to go back and change something that you now see as having gone in the wrong direction. Instead, keep a tablet nearby and jot down each point or question as it comes to you, or keep a separate file on the

---

*Time lines*

While writing the book, it may also help to create a time line of when events happened and who was where at what time. This will help keep you from having a character magically relocate or be in two places at once.

---

computer for this purpose. I also insert brackets ([ ]) into the ongoing text wherever I need a reminder. Sometimes the brackets contain a question—[Is this correct? Did I already mention this?]—or an instruction—[Follow up on this!]—and sometimes they're empty because I'm missing information. In any case, once the draft is finished—and only after it's finished—I have the computer search for brackets so I can find each trouble spot and work with it.

Avoid the temptation to revise before you complete the draft, unless the revisions are so massive and complex that starting over is the only way to unscramble your thinking and get on with it. It's sad but true that half the population has an unfinished manuscript in a desk drawer. Those incomplete works often have been polished to death, but they are still not books. Instead, wait until the draft is finished and then use your accumulated notes as a first guide to revision.

## TECHNICALLY SPEAKING
Write your book as if computers did not have fancy font options. Editors still prefer the old-fashioned way of indicating special type. For example, to indicate italic type, underline the word in roman (I won't give in) rather than switching to an italic font (I *won't* give in).

## HOW LONG SHOULD THE BOOK BE?
About now you may start to obsess about how long this book has to be. The obvious answer: as long as it takes to tell your story. But editors I consulted said that a manuscript that's approximately three hundred to four hundred pages is ideal for a crime novel. Joe Blades, associate publisher at Ballantine Books, said that nonseries novels, such as thrillers, are often longer. Remember, "longer" doesn't mean "padded."

Ruth Cavin, senior editor at St. Martin's Press, mentioned that the price of the published book depends on manuscript length, so they look for a "practical" length—between 300 and 350 pages. These numbers assume that a writer will use traditional and professional manuscript style—1½″ (3.8cm) margins on all four borders, printed on only one side of the paper and double-spaced in a traditional font. This will produce somewhere in the vicinity of 250–300 words per page.

But for now, just write your story. Later you can tinker with it and tighten it until you find its correct length, which, odds are, will be in the ballpark of three hundred pages.

## MIDBOOK BLUES

There is almost always a sagging time midbook, as you are pushing forward toward the climax, and you feel like Sisyphus with that impossible boulder and unclimbable hill. If you understand that this lack of energy is a nearly inevitable midbook malaise, you may find the courage to slog on.

If you feel absolutely stuck and that boulder gets more and more unmovable, consider skipping over it and writing the next scene you can envision—generally the big, climactic one.

Sometimes you'll discover you couldn't write those intermediate scenes because they didn't need to be written. The book is fine without them. Mentioning their planned content in passing elsewhere will probably suffice.

The scene you zoom forward to might, instead, be what feels like the conclusion of the book, in which all ends are tied up. In this instance, write a Perry Mason–like wrap-up and explain the crime. This will not end up in your draft, but it might help clarify the story and give you a handle on what has yet to be written.

If none of this works, remember the adage "Don't write it right, write it down." I have found that too often, I absolutely have to write the wrong chapter—go off on the wrong tack—before I can see the error of my ways and, only then, see a better way. It's not an efficient way to write, but it works.

Take heart—shortly ahead is the top of the mountain you're climbing, and once you reach the summit, it's a downhill breeze to home.

# 13 BRINGING CHARACTERS TO LIFE

Once you have a sense of your characters, how do you transmit it to your readers?

Sometimes, despite the adage "Show, don't tell," you may need to tell. Some of what the reader needs in order to form an image of your character—such as name, gender, age, general appearance, race or nationality, class, historic period and region—might not logically come up in conversation. The statistical, factual information might need to be told. It's best to set the scene as quickly as possible so that the reader can easily enter your world. If you're writing a series, this has to be done subtly and creatively with each new book.

Keep telling to a minimum and to facts. *Show* us attributes such as temper, wit and intelligence through dialogue, actions and thoughts.

## CHARACTERIZATION EXTENDS THROUGHOUT THE BOOK
Your reader immediately requires a few (significant) physical details that produce both an image and an emotional take on how he should feel about this person, not the entire portrait. The reader will fill in the blanks. Remember, too, you'll have the entire novel in which to enrich the characterization. It need not, should not, be in a single lump at the beginning, and it should be constantly refreshed throughout the novel. For example, Julie Smith's Skip Langdon is always going to define herself by her height. It's a part of her personality. She's been raised to be overly aware that her size and weight don't fit Southern belle specs, so throughout the book, there is a sense, whenever it's relevant, of how her comfort level with her size affects her movement,

agility and interactions with others. You have much more than one shot at description, so don't cram everything in at once. Instead, play-act as this character throughout so that you remember those physical attributes and consider how they'd affect everything in life.

And remember, if your sleuth is going to use sophisticated and special skills to get out of a pinch, subtly but definitely establish that she has such skills or background early on, before she needs them.

## FIRST IMPRESSIONS: THE FIVE SENSES

You needn't feel restricted to the eye/hair color cliché to describe any-one. People are much more than "green-eyed blondes." We learn about life through our five senses, and your readers will learn about the life on your pages the same way. Even though we aren't supposed to judge books by their covers, first impressions do count. In fiction and life, we deduce what sort of person is before us from the clues he provides. Give only a few details—the ones that stand out, that dominate, that tell your reader and your detective something about this person.

The way your character designs himself is revealing. Your detective should be aware, as should you, of the meaning of hair's cut and color; clothing's fit, cut, design and condition; makeup and accessories. Better than characterizing by brand names, try to convey the object's significance—the shiny worn fabric or lush softness of the wool, the weight of the gold watch that keeps her from lifting her arm too often. Your characters's "costumes" make statements of political, economic, religious, sexual, social and intellectual values.

The parts nature shaped (or surgery enhanced) are many, varied and potentially revealing of character. The face is full of options. Consider its general shape; the texture and appearance of the skin; the existence of moles, scars or wrinkles; and yes, those ever described windows to the soul, the eyes. Convey not only their color (and not the volumes to be read inside them), but also their spacing, size, expression. Determine the size and shape of the character's body and other features—eyebrows, nose, mouth, teeth, hair, forehead, chin and ears.

Michael Connelly presents the following characterizations in *The Black Echo*:

> Detectives Pierce Lewis and Don Clarke strode into the office and presented themselves. Neither spoke. They could have been brothers. They shared close-cropped brown hair,

the arms splayed build of weight lifters, conservative gray silk suits. Lewis's had a thin charcoal stripe, Clarke's maroon. Each man was built wide and low to the ground for better handling. Each had a slightly forward tilt to his body, as if he were wading out to sea, crashing through breakers with his face.

This description uses the detectives' lack of individuality in body type, haircut, suit style and stance. It also gives us a sense of their conservatism, via their choice of attire, and their pugnacious menace, through the imagery Connelly chooses to describe them.

Some of the above is about tactile attributes—the characters' general energy level (they "strode") and posture. Think also about possible nervous tics or gestures, gracefulness or clumsiness, facial expression. Consider a limp or crushing handshake, a soft belly or muscle-bound physique. Consider as well auditory attributes: a shrieked, brayed or melodic laugh; a stiff manner of speech, a boom or a whisper. And don't forget the sense of smell; you'd react emotionally to someone overdosed with perfume—or body odor.

We also influence our environment and put our stamp on our private spaces, so you can characterize someone via the condition or decor of his home, drawers, closets, car, office space.

Next time you're attracted to or repulsed by a person, consider which details so affected you. Remember them so you can use them in your fiction.

### Use a few significant details

You only need a few attributes—enough to give us a sense of the person and how we should feel about them. In *Lonely Hearts* by John Harvey, a character is described as: "whey- faced . . . with heavy-framed glasses and a decided stoop." His suit is said to be expensive, but worn with no style. Harvey goes on to say that:

> [his] hand was damp and cloying and Resnick was reminded of squeezing the water from spinach, cooked and rinsed.

Look how well a few excellent details filled with emotional resonance work. All we know of this man is his skin color, his posture, his need for glasses, his probable affluence, his sloppiness and his

81

flaccid handshake. We imagine a less-than-heroic man, not particularly attractive, sexy or dynamic.

## FIRST PERSON PROBLEMS

The device of the face in the mirror as a method of describing a character is clichéd, but it can be tempting, especially in first person narratives, and particularly as a series progresses, as its protagonist needs to be re-introduced with each book. If you use it, be sure you give emotional information along with a few features. Having another character comment on the narrator's appearance—either because he looks changed or because he doesn't—or having the narrator tell us directly is easier than trying to make the mirror approach work. For expediency's sake, I'll use examples from my Amanda Pepper series. The first, from *Philly Stakes*, is somebody else's description (more or less) of Amanda.

> Two months ago, I found one of Clemmy's works tacked to my bulletin board. It was a remarkably comprehensive full-color portrait of a tall woman with long red-brown hair, a recognizable nose and eyes much greener than mine actually are. The blackboard behind her said, "Foxy English Teacher." The body, centerfold material and exquisitely detailed, was extremely flattering and the most imaginative work Clemmy had ever done in my classroom. Still, I had problems dealing with the fact that, aside from a volume of Shakespeare in the woman's hand and stiletto high heels on her feet, she was stark naked.

Amanda describes herself (more or less) in this example from *With Friends Like These . . .*

> Sometimes I look at my mother and see myself, gently distorted as in, perhaps, a kindly fun-house mirror. She is smaller, rounder, her features not truly mine, but definitely their source. We both have precisely the same auburn hue on our heads, although now hers is mostly chemical. She achieved the match by holding up swatches of my hair— my head still attached—to every box of chestnut, auburn, brown, and red dye in the pharmacy.

Unassisted nature made our eyes the same confused green, which a seriously yuppified acquaintance described as the color of overhandled money. But whatever their tint, there is a horrific optimistic innocence in my mother's eyes that I hope is missing in mine.

Once you've thought through your characters and you're living through the action with them, slow down and live in their skin. Become an actor; wear the mask of this other person and look through his eyes. The details that are selected and the reaction to them depends on who is making note of them. Think "Does what I see or hear or am made aware of reflect something in my own life and background? Something I want or fear or hate? If I've spent my entire life feeling poor and needy, will I be more prone to noticing—and disapproving of—what seems excess, showy or frivolous in others?"

What would a professional thief notice in a house? A homicide detective? A decorator? A homeless person? These things will give indications of both the observed and observing characters' personalities.

## ACTIONS AND REACTIONS

Actions speak at least as loudly as words. This includes reactions.

By his deeds you shall know him. Emotion produces physical reactions, some of which end with murder—and mysteries about them. Study the wide range of human mannerisms. This is another way to use otherwise dreary waits at the airport, bus stop and service counter. Body language, not the spoken word, is said to make up 65 percent of our communication. The writer has to be aware of the nonverbal ways we convey emotion. We stand back or lean into people. We pound tables, tap fingers, fiddle with hair, wrinkle brows, frown, let our eyes wander, cross our arms, cower. The list goes on and on, each action signifying an emotional reaction to a situation.

Slow down and consider what your point-of-view character is experiencing. Is the gun heavy in her hands? Its kick painful? Is it hard to lift the cudgel—does something in his back clench or twang?

Verbs express action, so why use only generic ones? Why say that someone entered and crossed a room in order to stand in front of a desk when you can use the language to put it this way, so much more vividly and with so much more characterization:

Before I could finish my sentence, my office door flew open and Stewart McClaren burst inside. He sauntered across the room, a lean, cool study in denim and leather, and planted himself in front of my drawing table.
—Marilyn Wallace, *The Seduction*

Notice how we have an immediate image of McClaren, primarily through kinetic verbs—the door "flew" open, the man "burst" in, he "sauntered" and "planted" himself. We feel as if we immediately know him and see him when his personality is showing via verbs.

Look at the specifics of appearance and behavior around you. Mentally squint, almost as if you had to caricature the person, capture his entire essence with a few lines of his dominant, defining characteristics. Those go onto the page to form a clear, convincing image.

# 14 TALK ABOUT DIALOGUE

One of your best power tools is your character's own voice. As with all aspects of fiction, we'll try to give the impression of reality, not copy it, because real-life talk is anything but dramatic. Real-life conversation is dull, disjointed, meandering. ("So it's like, um, I'm not saying, you know, not good, but kind of, not exactly terrific. More sort of, well, boring, actually.") It can have almost no content and be no more than a sociably acceptable way of filling time or putting others at ease ("Nice day, isn't it?" "And have you known the bride for long?") or serve only to impart information ("Please pass the mustard." "Are you in this line?").

None of this has tension.

## DIALOGUE HAS THREE FUNCTIONS

Good dialogue boils real speech down to its flavorful essence, while performing three functions at once. As in real life, dialogue provides information. Again, as in real life, the choice of words and the manner in which they're said reveal/reflect character. But unlike much of real life, dialogue also moves things along, advancing your story line.

Good dialogue is action. Think of it as arrows shot at someone with a purpose—to hurt, inform, spite, confuse, delight, seduce, and so forth. And no arrow should be wasted.

One aspect of actual talk we can adopt is its lack of eloquence. Don't make your characters too smooth-talking unless you want us to be suspicious of them, because they'll sound as if they're reciting prepared speeches.

Your mystery has a lot of back story. Deciphering that hidden story is the mystery. Nonetheless, old information needn't be presented through clumsy dialogue. To illustrate, let's invent characters: Velma, Gladys and Humphrey.

This is bad dialogue and is not the way people—real or fictional—convey past history:

> "Ever since my treacherous fiancé, Humphrey, tried to force himself on you, my sister, and in a fit of anger I killed him and we buried him near the roses, I can't sleep or eat because I'm so afraid that the gardener will dig Humphrey up and our secret will be revealed. I'm so nervous being with you because I don't trust you. No matter what you say, I'm still not sure whether Humphrey was seducing you or you were after him to ruin everything for me because you resented my engagement from day one."

If we need to know any of that for story sense, we have to use other, better ways.

You can be direct, and tell us these facts in your narrative voice.

> Seven days earlier, when Velma returned from volunteer work at the hospital, she found her fiancé, Humphrey, in his car in a more than compromising position with her sister Gladys and clubbed him to death with his antitheft device. With her sister's assistance, Velma buried him in the back of the garden. This was the one time in their lives the sisters could recall cooperating with one another.

A speaker can believably repeat information the listener knows if the information answers a question or requires emphasis. For example:

> "Oh, Gladys, every time that gardener heads for the roses, I shake and—"
>
> "You sniveling coward. Humphrey's behind the rosebushes, not under them."
>
> "The gardener will notice the mound."
>
> "Then fire the gardener and do the work yourself. I'm sick of your whining!"
>
> "If you said you did it in self-defense, that you killed him because your own sister's fiancé was raping you, no jury would—"

"I did it? You're not framing me! I was in no position to do anything to the back of his head, was I? You pulled that thing off the steering wheel, you conked him on the head, you—"

If a speaker is giving a listener information the listener doesn't need, then the speaker must be saying these things out of a need of his own. Velma is falling apart and needs reassurance and calming down, and she also wants to convince Gladys that she shared in the crime and should plead guilty to murder.

Gladys needs to set the record (as she sees it) straight. Angry people—on and off the page—tend to dredge up old material and hurl it at each other. Again, human beings speak out of their own needs, not necessarily the needs of their listeners.

Both Gladys's hands were tight fists. "Since the day you were born, you've been out of control, and I'm sick of it! Whatever you want, you get. Whatever it takes—crying, tantrums, hunger strikes. When you wanted a bunny rabbit, you got it. When you didn't want the bunny anymore—"

"Will you ever stop harping on that bunny? It was twenty-five years—"

"When you wanted your own convertible, you got it. I got a bus pass! Whatever you wanted—"

"Stop it! This time you got what you wanted—you were the one who wanted to bury him in our own backyard!"

## SPEECH REFLECTS THE SPEAKER

Your character's words mean something, but vocabulary choices and speech patterns should simultaneously suggest personality or emotion and reflect all you know about that person. Might he skip certain parts of speech, qualify every phrase, sound like a telegram or an orator? Does he talk without pause until he's breathless, or is he stingy with words? Less-than-secure people might end sentences with questions—"Don't you think so?" "Isn't it?"

Think about the roles people play and have yours speak accordingly. Do you have a yes-man? A negotiator? A smoother-over? An agitator? A confrontational devil's advocate? A timid, fearful, noncommittal type? Each would shape different sentences.

87

As your sleuth goes about the business of detecting, remember that just because someone's speaking doesn't necessarily mean he wants to be informative or revealing. His choice of words might be influenced by a desire to confuse, hurt, evade or seduce. He might need to establish a relationship or a hierarchy of power or to present himself a certain way. Again, you aren't writing the story of a sleuth and a bunch of cardboard figures. People being questioned don't necessarily want the same thing the detective wants. Write their dialogue accordingly.

Most of the time people do *not* answer or listen to each other. A truly considered, logical response is rare. We answer from inside our own ongoing drama. Somebody says, "Help! I'm shot," and too often, the response is, "You think *you're* hurt? If you knew how bad a headache I have. . . . " Most so-called dialogues are really two monologues. This is another reason it's important to know lots about your characters. They are more than pegs in a plot, so keep in mind each private agenda, and avoid the knee-jerk syndrome in dialogue, too. Would your character answer logically and directly, or would he have a more instinctive, off-center, tension-producing response?

However well they listen and respond, they're going to react in unique ways depending on who they are. A simple question like "How are you?" could evoke:

"What's it to you?"
—or—
"Great. Absolutely great. Never felt better. Ever since I discovered Vitamin Z, I've—"
—or—
"Not too bad."
—or—
"Don't even ask."
—or—
"Like you really care."
—or—
"Happy, now that you're finally paying attention to me, babe."
—or—
"It's so sweet of you to ask!"

And so on. Live inside your characters' skins and let each have his own sound, just as we do in life. That way, your dialogue will constantly reveal and reflect character.

In almost any mystery, at least one important character—most notably the victim—might never have a chance to reveal his own character. We come to know him by what others say about him and by the record of his past actions. But remember to enrich your living players' characterizations by the reactions of other people to them.

## SUMMARIZED, INDIRECT AND DIRECT DIALOGUE

Fictional characters start conversations in the middle, skipping the irrelevant-to-the-story parts. They stop talking when they've made their point. All irrelevant but sociable chitchat can be *summarized*.

> Gladys and the sheriff's deputy, both ill at ease, stood near the rose garden and made gardener-to-gardener talk for a half an hour.

If you want a more specific sense of their chat, you can use *indirect dialogue*.

> Gladys and the sheriff's deputy talked about problems they'd been having with thrips and root mold and listed hybrids they'd been cultivating in their gardens. Turned out he'd been working on creating a yellow and apricot variety for seven years now.

But when something dramatic and relevant happens—when there's an element of conflict, and specific words and how they are said matter to your story—use *direct dialogue*.

> "Ma'am?" he said after clearing his throat. "Fascinating as garden talk is, fact is, I'm here at your rose garden on official business. We have a report. Seems your gardener—"
> "Former gardener. The man's been fired."
> "—spotted a man's hand back by the American beauties."

You can mix these techniques. Sue Grafton does that in *"A" is for Alibi*, saving direct dialogue for two lines:

> She was a chatty little thing, full of pep, and I wondered if she wasn't about perfect for Henry Pitts. Since Charlie

Scorsoni was keeping me waiting, I took my revenge by eliciting as much information from Ruth as I could manage without appearing too rude. She told me she had worked for Scorsoni and Powers since the formation of their partnership seven years ago. Her husband had left her for a younger woman (fifty-five) and Ruth, on her own for the first time in years, had despaired of ever finding a job, as she was then sixty-two years old, "though in perfect health," she said. She was quick, capable, and of course was being aced out at every turn by women one-third her age who were cute instead of competent.

"The only cleavage I got left, I sit on," she said and then hooted at herself.

Use dialect sparingly if at all. Suggest it rather than cause the reader to stop and work at a misspelled word. Use syntax, an occasional idiomatic phrase, a word here and there and minimal spelling changes. Be sparing with slang and professional jargon.

If you've chosen first person as your point of view, then remember that your novel is a book-length monologue by your narrator. Once the draft is done and revised, read the entire book into a tape recorder, then settle back and listen. Does every bit of it sound the way your narrator would speak?

## DIRECT ADDRESS, DIALOGUE AND TONAL TAGS: CAUTION—USE SPARINGLY

Don't overuse direct address. We don't in real life. Does this sound believable?

"Oh, Gladys, whenever I see that gardener, I can barely breathe."

"Don't be such a coward, Velma. Humphrey's not under the roses."

"I know, Gladys, but that mound . . . he'll see it and—"

"I swear, Velma! If it bothers you that much, get out there and do the gardening yourself!"

"But, Gladys, if you'd say you did it because he was raping you, a jury would—"

"Me? I should say I did it? Are you out of your mind, Velma?"

Here's another bad option. This time, we'll be overly generous with dialogue tags.

> "Whenever I see that gardener, I can barely breathe," Velma gasped.
>
> "Don't be such a coward," Gladys snapped. "Humphrey's not under the roses."
>
> "I know," moaned Velma, "but that mound . . . he'll see it and—"
>
> "I swear!" Gladys swore, "If it bothers you that much, get out there and do the gardening yourself!"
>
> "But if you'd say you did it because he was raping you," Velma whined, "a jury would—"
>
> "Me?" Gladys shrieked. "I should say I did it? Are you out of your mind, Velma?"

Use *said*—it's invisible—but don't use it every single time in a back-and-forth conversation. Who else would Velma be addressing? Who else would be answering? Skip most tags, and use one only when you're afraid the reader might be losing hold of who is speaking. Even then, you can omit the identifying tag altogether if the character does something physical at the same time.

> "Whenever I see that gardener, I can barely breathe." Velma dug her nails into the soft wood of the windowsill.

The action goes on the same line as the dialogue and is linked to it, indicating that the speaker and the actor are one and the same.

Use tonal tags sparingly. They are tellings. In " 'I hate you!' Velma screamed angrily," do we need either the "screamed" or the "angrily"? If the emotion is obvious from the words, don't be redundant. Let dialogue itself convey the tone. If the dialogue doesn't tell us enough about the manner in which the words were said, an action will often do so better than an adverb.

> "I hate you!" She hurled a vase, her sister's favorite, and smiled as it smashed against the wall.

## LET THE READER HEAR IMPORTANT DIALOGUE

Using dialogue where appropriate is also a part of playing fair with the reader. Nothing is more frustrating than to be told something significant was heard rather than to hear it. How infuriating would it be to read, for example, "And then she said it, the words that made all the difference, and I finally knew what had driven Gladys to crime"? Don't do that. Your readers want to live the story, see it. They don't want to be told about it, and they certainly don't want to be deliberately left out of it.

## DEALING WITH BLOCKS OF INFORMATION

You'll often reach a point where great chunks of information need to be said, either to explain a process or to unravel part of the mystery. Your dialogue is in danger of sounding like a speech, not conversation, and of becoming stagnant because data isn't action and has no tension. See if some of the material could be conveyed earlier, as part of the sleuthing process, or held back a while longer. Then, add tension to whatever's left. Perhaps one character wants to talk about it, and the other is too impatient or distracted to listen or thinks he already knows whatever is going to be said. Or maybe you can break up the flow of information with an interruption—a secondary story line's intrusion, a telephone interruption, a frustratingly friendly or inept waiter. Sometimes a physical prop helps, but use it to further the larger action or delineate the character. When a character gets up and looks out the window or pours another drink, the reader doesn't know (or care) that you are trying to apply CPR to your exposition-heavy scene. He expects that if it's on the page, it's significant, and it's showing us something about her—that she's a snoop or nervous about something outside, that she's a drunk or hiding something. Don't cheat or annoy the reader; make your prop work and make it fit.

Don't repeat information the reader already knows even if a new character needs to know it. If the new character is going to react to the news in an important way, summarize the telling of it ("She told him what had happened to Humphrey") or give one sentence of the news ("Velma killed Humphrey," she said, and then she explained how she'd done it). The point is to let us know only that the new guy knows.

Avoid great stretches of unbroken dialogue with no narration or action interrupting it. It may feel as if it's clipped and fast that way, but it actually cuts off all our senses except our ears—we "go blind" listening to the story.

Writers can read minds, which makes fiction more fun than life, and thoughts can enrich the action and dialogue. The methods of presenting them are close to those of presenting dialogue, without the quotation marks enclosing it.

## BRING DIALOGUE TO LIFE VIA WORD CHOICE, ACTIONS AND THOUGHT

To make the most out of your dialogue, remember you have a variety of techniques available to make it as rich and resonant as possible.

Here's information with an underwhelming amount of conflict or tension:

> "Oh, Gladys, where have you been? The gardener called. I'm all shaky."
>
> Gladys came in and put her packages down. "Freeway was stalled. I sat in traffic from the Trippedy Rock exit on."
>
> "Slippery Rock," Velma said.
>
> "Whatever. I'm tired."
>
> "I'm nervous."

Here's the same exchange with tension put into the dialogue itself:

> "You took your good time about getting home," Velma said when Gladys opened the front door. "You knew I'd worry, and I had good reason. The gardener called. He . . . he sounded funny, like he was going to . . . do something."
>
> "What's he going to do? Fertilize the perennial bed? Oooh, scary."
>
> "Blackmail us. Where *were* you?"
>
> "Stuck in traffic, not whipping up paranoid fantasies the way you were. Accident around Trippedy Rock."
>
> "Slippery Rock, for God's sake. Why do you insist on baby talk? You're middle aged!"
>
> "I thought you were worried about blackmail, not my vocabulary."

And here's conflict added through action and thought with the same words as in the first version:

> "Oh, Gladys, where have you been? The gardener called. I'm all shaky."
>
> Gladys put her packages down, one by one. Tissue and fragrances pushed their way out of the four shiny, paper

93

department totes. She looked as if she'd had someone shop for her while she lounged at a spa. She examined her nails, which were newly scarlet. They seemed her only concern.

Velma put her own hands with their bitten nails behind her back. Her sister grew harder and slicker every day while she dissolved into ragged-edged mush.

"Freeway was stalled," Gladys said. "I sat in traffic from the Trippedy Rock exit on."

"Slippery Rock." Her sister's affectations made her crazy. Baby talk out of that mean middle-aged mouth. Still thought she was precious. Mummy's pweshus widdle murderer.

"Whatever." Gladys, overacting as always, yawned extravagantly. "I'm tired."

And senile. And deaf. Hadn't she heard anything? The gardener knew. You could tell from his tone. "I'm nervous," Velma said, hoping her sister's hearing would improve.

Tension doesn't have to be antagonistic, either. This scene could be rewritten with Velma saying the same words out of a different set of emotions—a troubled but loving concern for her sister's mental health and future. It's all up to you.

## THE INCONSISTENT TRAIT

In presenting your characters, choose from your full arsenal—appearance, dialogue, thoughts, actions and environment—showing what's possible and telling us the facts that won't otherwise be naturally conveyed. Be aware that we are comfortable with people who seem "of a piece." That is, their appearance, speech, background and environment seem consistent with one another.

Inconsistency—what doesn't fit—feels odd or frightening. As writers, we can see and use that discordant note, even if it's as silent as a thought. A calm exterior and a violent word obsessively playing in the mind. An elegant wardrobe and a stevedore's vocabulary. Words of reassurance with a hand shaking too badly to offer a glass of water. A killer performing his gory acts with a clear, even serene, mind. The jarring detail might also serve as a clue to the sleuth who notices it, but in any case, the imbalance produces tension. Just make sure that once the mystery of your character's background is revealed, the piece that appears to not fit actually does.

# 15 NOW YOU SEE IT, NOW YOU DON'T: HIDING CLUES

I've mentioned the mystery writer's duty to play fair. This translates into having the reader know all information the detective knows and know it at the same time.

Remember that the mystery, among other things, is a contest between the reader and the sleuth as to who will unravel the puzzle first. It's a game the reader wants to lose, but he doesn't want to be duped. Ideally, your detective will make sense of what he's learned just before your reader does, and your reader will be both surprised—he hadn't realized such and such (although he can now see how he should have)—and delighted.

## A CLUE IN EVERY CHAPTER

The unraveling of the clues provides much of the basic framework of your novel, so try to have each chapter/scene frame a clue. This will also move your story along. We grow closer to the goal of revealing the murderer with each clue—unless, of course, it's not a valid clue at all, or worse, a red herring. The actual red herring was smoked, then dragged across the trail to distract hunting dogs from their objective. Fictional red herrings serve the same purpose: They suggest attractive prey, a trail to follow, but ultimately, that trail leads nowhere and has no significance. You can certainly have a number of suspects and sinister seeming clues that turn out to be innocuous. Build them into the plot. But don't use many red herrings. Such ominous and powerful material that has no significance to the story is just plain annoying.

Worth mentioning again is that playing fair includes good manners and consideration for your splendid readers. Shun such ploys as having your sleuth say she knows something but not say what it is. Or having her fail to mention a piece of vital information she was given. Or having the mystery's solution depend on esoteric information that's never explained in the text, so your reader couldn't possibly be expected to make sense of it. Or any variation thereof.

But then, one might wonder how to share everything and still practice the legerdemain that's necessary to bamboozle those clever readers.

## DIVERTING THE READER'S ATTENTION

Basically, you use the magician's trick of distracting the eye. If the writer draws attention by emphasizing one thing while the actual item of future importance, the embryonic clue, is given less or incorrect emphasis, the reader is apt to glide right over the important item and/ or its significance.

> "Look at that vase. Must have cost a million dollars," Gladys said.
>
> I looked at the mantelpiece, but there was nothing but photographs of generations of Madame Latousse's homely family. I looked at the cluttered whatnot, but there was nothing but a collection of porcelain birds, mostly raptors—hawks and one Maltese falcon. Finally, I spotted the vase. I have no idea why it took me that long to notice it— it was four feet tall and filled with peacock feathers.

If it weren't a Maltese falcon, would you have noticed it enough to have it register? It's what will eventually have to be recalled and its significance grasped, but you're looking for the vase.

A clue can be nearly anything—action, gesture, movement, speech pattern, attire—particularly if, in a subtle manner, it does not go with the way the person presents himself or his history. If you give each of your characters human flaws and inconsistencies, they'll seem more realistic. This will also help disguise the fatal flaw and inconsistency in the killer.

Clues can also be via analogy, when the sleuth and the reader see something not particularly related to the case, but only the sleuth makes the connection. Miss Marple was a whiz at this. Everybody, including the reader, saw the goings-on in St. Mary Mead, but only she also saw enough of human nature in those goings-on to understand how they applied to crime.

## HIDING IN PLAIN SIGHT

One good technique is planting vital information *before* it can be applied. If matter-of-factly we learn something about a character before he turns into a corpse or killer, we don't necessarily have the frame of reference in which to see its significance and store it away. Only in retrospect can the dots be connected, and that's a feat of cleverness (and total recall) at which our sleuths excel. Sometimes, the function of the first few chapters is to plant those clues before we know enough to notice them.

Give the item spin. Make the fact seem to serve a different purpose than you know it does. I sometimes try, in the Amanda Pepper series, to use humor to misdirect. I want the reader to smile, move on and not realize that what was just said has significance beyond its amusement factor.

Have your protagonist misinterpret the meaning of the clue. After all, clues are merely facts selected out of the blizzard of sensory data that bombards us, the difference being their significance. Therefore, if the sleuth makes note of the fact, but not yet of its meaning, you've played fair.

If you can break your clue into several parts and scatter the pieces, you'll make it that much more difficult for the reader to grasp their significance as a unit. The example below attempts that.

Because I'm about to commit the crime of revealing clues that are meant to be hidden, I'm going to quote from my own writing. However, to minimize the self-inflicted damage, I'm going to use clues not to the killer's identity, but to how the unarmed Amanda will save her own life in *The Mummers' Curse.*

Since I'm trying to play fair, the reader has to learn along with Amanda that aerosol cans can become torches if they're put too close to a flame. But I don't want to have that fact register as something significant to hang onto. So long before she's going to need to apply this knowledge, while taking roll at school after winter break, Amanda notes three students absent: one with the flu; one who missed her plane back to Philadelphia; and one, "Badluck" Dooney Scott—so named because of his propensity to mess up—burned as a result of trying to see whether an aerosol can's warning to "keep away from open flame" meant anything. Amanda doesn't believe a word of it. She's sure that in reality, all three are extending tropical winter vacations. Underpaid, under-tropically-vacationed, she resents them. This is structured to make you pay more attention to the teacher's miseries than to what you've just read about aerosols.

Later in the novel, it's made clear that Amanda's pocketbook is oversized and that all manner of things (including a planted gun, at one point) find their way into it.

And then, near the end of the book, she's on a dark, deserted street, unable to find her car keys, and she dumps the pocketbook's contents onto the car's hood and catalogs the results.

> I removed flotsam. My emergency stuck-in-a-line book of short stories; a folding hairbrush; a plastic container of mints; the small can of hair spray I lugged all over and had used only to immobilize a yellowjacket trying to carpool with me; five lipsticks; countless pens; two matchbooks. I hadn't smoked in well over a year, but matchbooks were how I remembered good restaurants. At home, I tossed them into a large bowl. Rooting through it was like having a dining-out Rolodex.
>
> I removed the ubiquitous packet of fraying three-by-fives, neatly wrapped in a rubber band. A rupturing audio-cassette. A container of floss and a still-wrapped toothbrush from my last visit to the dentist. My roll book.
>
> No keys. Even with the bag half-empty, I could neither see, nor hear, nor touch their comforting metal.

I'm trying to make you worry about her inability to find her keys, about the potential danger of her being on the deserted street, unable to get into her car. Possibly about what a mess is in her pocketbook, too. To distract your attention further, she is put under attack and in great jeopardy by a masked, costumed someone.

Therefore, when she ultimately is inspired to fabricate a firebomb, I hope to surprise the reader—but to have played fair. I've told him everything Amanda knew—that aerosol sprays can be set on fire and burn people, and that she has a can of hair spray as well as matches in her pocketbook.

The spray can mentioned above is in the middle of the long list of her pocketbook's contents, and that was deliberately done. The middle of anything—a chapter, a paragraph, a sentence—is the weakest, most ignorable spot. If Amanda had pulled out the spray can first or last, it would be much more likely to stick in the reader's mind. So bury more than the body—bury the clues as well.

Sometimes, the clue is what didn't happen or wasn't said or isn't there. There is, ever and always, Conan Doyle's dog that didn't bark in the night. Another example is in Dorothy L. Sayers's *Five Red Herrings*, where there's a catalog of paint tubes on the ground near an artist's easel. Lots and lots of colors, and the tendency of the reader is to skim through the list because there's no special significance attached to any one of the colors. But while the painting on the easel has lots of clouds, there's no white paint on the floor. Ergo, the painting was done somewhere else, possibly by someone else. But who made note of that missing paint tube at the time?

You can also hide clues in plain sight. Suppose your victim was killed by a blunt instrument which is missing from the scene. Plunk a lot of blunt instruments within the grasp of suspects throughout the novel: a ball peen hammer; a granite countertop waiting to be installed; a rolling pin; a frozen leg of lamb, as in the classic Roald Dahl episode on *Alfred Hitchcock Presents*; a Maltese falcon. Show, perhaps, something that has endured a blunt instrument: a piece of hammered metal art in a workshop, tenderized beef.

If you then add a time problem—where that granite countertop was at the time of the murders, who had that Maltese falcon then, and so forth—then, in working that out, you'll have lots of smoke and mirrors in which to bury the clue that represents the true weapon, and it will be done as part of real, ongoing, natural action.

Something hidden in plain sight can be an incongruous element that's given simply, then reconsidered. As a visual equivalent of this, an early episode of the TV series *Homicide: Life on the Street* had a missing blonde suspect. Only later (after we'd seen mug shots) did a detective realize that the eyebrows of one of the suspects were too light. His hair had been dyed dark, but he was, indeed, the missing blonde man.

Another trick is based on the fact that if you tell somebody to watch out for something, he will seldom be able to recall whatever immediately preceded the watched-for item. Perhaps your detective will say it's important to determine whether someone is left-handed. Then you show a suspect using her left hand to write, but immediately before that happens, you put in whatever you want to slip past your reader.

Another distractor would be major action immediately after a clue's been presented. In the chase or confusion or excitement that follows, your clue will fade in the reader's mind.

## TRACK THE CLUES YOU'VE LEFT

If you're writing your book in third person from more than one point of view, be careful about who knows what. It is possible that you're increasing tension by having the reader aware of something the sleuth can't know. That's good, but, at the risk of stating the obvious, make sure that the sleuth isn't basing her solution on that information.

One helpful hint is to take a printout of the draft of your manuscript and highlight clues you've planted and need to follow up or explain. This will make it easier to be sure you've done so.

# 16 WITH A LITTLE HELP FROM MY FRIENDS

There comes a time when you have written, revised, tinkered and pondered to the point where you've lost the ability to judge your work objectively. If you aren't already part of a workshop or critique group and aren't receiving thoughtful feedback, this is a good time to seek input on how closely you've communicated your vision.

This is a terrifying step. Nobody likes to be criticized. Acknowledge that and move on. Writers need to be brave.

## GROUND RULES FOR CRITIQUE GROUPS

You may want to join a writing group or class or to form one. In either case, be sure it's organized and designed to help fulfill your writing potential and it is neither a support group disguised as a critique group nor a destructive group designed to squelch and intimidate. If you wind up in either of these situations, leave.

The page, not the author, is critiqued. The goal is to make this effort work as best it can—not to decide whether this work should exist or whether this author should write.

You can be part of a general workshop in which people write in a variety of genres as long as your fellow members don't have a hierarchy of what is worth writing. You want the participants to accept your mystery on its own terms.

Ignore comments that aim to rewrite or rethink your basic concept ("I just don't want to read about murder") and critics who want you to sound more like Agatha Christie or John Grisham—or themselves. The ideal group accepts the spirit and intention of your story and tries only to decide whether it accomplished what you wanted it to do. And the group does so specifically, in a way that helps you rethink any problem.

The critiquing you do in return is not selfless. As you progress from "I didn't like it" toward an analysis of what works and why, you're teaching yourself to edit.

Unfortunately, it's easier to spot problems than to solve them. Therefore, pay attention to what's critiqued, but don't immediately jump at the solutions your group might make. Give yourself time to sift through them and find your own way.

I believe that reading the manuscript in advance and writing out responses is infinitely more valuable than hearing it read out loud and immediately responding. What you get via comments written at home is your readers' first take on the writing, not a possibly false tidal wave of echoes and me-too's.

Workshop time is then used for discussing manuscripts, not listening to them. More work can be critiqued in one session, and this matters when you're writing a novel.

However, this requires advanced preparation and expense, since the group should all receive copies of your submission one meeting before the one where it's to be critiqued.

Even if your group decides to read aloud, consider giving each member a copy of the portion being critiqued so it can be consulted as needed. Otherwise, every time the listener reflects on what's read or makes a note, he misses whatever's being read next. Also, the reader has to beware dramatic readings that add emotion that isn't on the page itself. Have someone other than the author read the work in as flat a tone as possible so that the words do all the work.

## FRAMING A CRITIQUE

Begin your critique by noting what *did* work. The author needs to know this, too. A check in the margin indicating special praise is almost as good as a check in the mail. Try to make your first two points statements of what is positive. Be kind. Remember that every writer's ego is as fragile as yours and never gets any stronger.

Be as specific as possible. Rather than "I lost interest," which is in no way helpful, look at the manuscript and find what bothered you—why and at what point your mind wandered or your eyes skipped ahead—and say precisely that. It's much more useful to the writer to be told, "Around here, I became annoyed with John. I wanted him to finally notice what was going on and do something about it, and when he didn't, I stopped caring whether he was in danger." This allows the writer to assess his work and either justify John's obliviousness, change the situation, change John's behavior or decide you're all wrong. Jot notes in the margin if you "suspect this one's the murderer," even though you're on page 3. This will either alert the writer to a problem or please him because his red herrings are working.

Be honest. People deserve your true reaction. If you stick to the text and are specific, you will be helpful and not destructive.

You need not suggest remedies for problem areas, but you do need to clearly define what the problems are.

Write your critique. Make notes on the back of the manuscript, or type a critique. Think about what you're going to say. Don't rely on flipping through the manuscript looking for marginal notes. (Make those notes, but then summarize what your overall views are.) Don't become a yes-person, echoing what someone else said. In the first round, say only what you observed on your own.

Don't nitpick. Grammar, punctuation and spelling are important, but not the primary concern here. If such problems really interfere, say so and let it go. The writer who knows she has a problem should find someone who'll either swap services or be paid for editing.

If you feel the work can be tightened, say so. Suggest where and how. Line editing is time consuming; a few suggestions might suffice.

## BEING CRITIQUED

On the other side, he who is critiqued shall distribute his manuscript by the suggested deadline. The work should be ready for critiquing— that is, be as polished and complete as the writer can make it at the moment—so that the group's critique will be relevant and helpful rather than devoted to issues the writer knows he could have handled himself.

The person critiqued should acknowledge that he wants to hear, "This was perfect," but since few things are, his work is about to be criticized. Despite this, the writer should try to avoid becoming defensive. Listen to the comments. Tape-record them if you like. We tend to recall only the negatives, so a tape might surprise you afterwards with the positive comments that you mentally discarded.

Do not defend or explain your work during the first critique round. Let each reader speak in turn while you listen. Don't allow readers to comment on one another's critiques. Don't answer questions. This round will simply establish that questions exist. After that round you can ask for clarification, explain what you had intended, and open the discussion again so the group can more specifically address how the work met or failed to meet its own goals.

When submitting your manuscript, if you have a question that needs attention but might otherwise be overlooked, put a note at the *end* of the manuscript saying what specific points you want addressed. ("Did you understand that the baby in the gutter was a hallucination?" "Did Doris's behavior too obviously flag her secret?") That way you won't prejudice or skew your readers in advance.

If everybody disagrees on the meaning or intent of your work, it may be a sign not that they're stupid, but that your work is unfocused. Find a way to make your point clear.

Understand that within any group you will find opinions that seem rational and opinions that do not. Learn whose opinions you trust and politely ignore the critiques of those who don't ever seem in harmony with your take on writing.

But, as W.C. Fields said, "When enough people tell you you're drunk, it's time to sit down."

## ALTERNATIVES TO REAL-TIME GROUPS
If you can't find a group in your area, consider cyberspace. There are helpful on-line writing workshops and critique groups. Surf the Net for topics relating to writing—specifically, writing mysteries—and you'll undoubtedly find a few to test.

Aside from a group or class, real or virtual, other "friends" can help bring home the points made in this book. They are published writers, and they help via their books.

The next time you enjoy a mystery, do a second read and analyze how it was done. Where and how was tension introduced? Did it grab you immediately with a dramatic opening or with less overt drama but a sense of foreboding? How was that foreshadowing done?

How did the writer keep the tension mounting throughout? Try making a rough outline of what happens when. Note where the author placed the dramatic highlights and built to the climax. What was summarized and what was shown through scenes? Where did each chapter begin and end, and what was the job of that chapter? Did it pull you in? Did its ending make you turn the page for more? How?

How was the main character presented and developed? How much description was up front? Was it both physical description and emotional hints? How and where else did the author reinforce and add to that image?

How are thoughts and emotions shown?

How are the five senses used? What are the best details used?

Where does the story begin and end? Could it have started somewhere else? Does it move from start to finish with or without flashbacks or a frame?

Now that you know the solution, look for where and how the author planted clues.

Look for any points of craft that are mentioned in this book to see how they were achieved.

Even a book that fails to impress you can be helpful. Since you didn't fall in love with it, it's easier to notice its flaws. Before you hurl the book into the recycling pile, check back and see why and how the author fumbled.

And whatever he did, don't you do it!

# 17 WHAT DID YOU SAY?
## THE MACRO EDIT

Bravo! You've written a mystery.

Now you have a clearer sense of where you were going and of the villains, victims and sleuths making the voyage with you. Along the way, you may have hit dead, or comatose, plot ends, discovered new options, changed your take on a character or realized potentials that were invisible at the start. In short, anything could and probably did happen during the first draft, so what you've produced may be shaggy and unkempt with a head that doesn't in any way match its tail. Now's your chance to groom it into shape.

This is when we finally allow our critical selves back into the writing room, where they'll act as editors.

Take a deep breath and be grateful for the gift of revision, the chance to get it right. The ability to rewrite is what differentiates the amateur from the professional.

First, we'll do a macroedit: a consideration of the large, structural issues of your mystery; a refocusing. Here, you ask, "What was I trying to say or do, and did I say or do it?"

Revise whatever you can on the computer, but then do further revision from hard copy. Reading your words on the page is a subtly different process than reading them on the screen, and you will "hear" and note more. If you are in a critique group, the following points might also apply to critiquing manuscripts.

### BRIEFLY SUMMARIZE YOUR MYSTERY

Pretend you're writing a query letter to an agent who needs a snappy selling handle for editors with short attention spans. If you're using this for a critique group, don't show them the summary, but listen carefully to their responses to see if they get it.

Here's a summary of a hypothetical mystery:

> Driving along a country road, two teens accidentally kill a pedestrian, then, in a panic, bury the body. No one ever reports the person missing. The boy and girl keep their secret for years, even after they've gone their separate ways: he's become a politician; she, a reporter. Then, a housing project on the country site unearths the remains, and the pressure builds as the two of them are plunged into moral dilemmas that escalate into violence. The book is not only a puzzle, but an exploration of guilt and responsibility.

This may have been your idea from the start, or it may have emerged as you wrote. Now that you have it, consider your characters and see how they fit this premise. Are most involved in the questions of who-dunit and of guilt and responsibility? Without overstating it or making the novel preachy, could that aspect use underlining or heightening?

Take a look at the basic element of fiction—change. There is (we hope) the basic change from start to finish—the unsolved crime is now solved. But how about other aspects? Does another change relate to the premise and therefore have something to do with your exploration of guilt and responsibility? Go through the steps of change. Where are the boy and girl morally, emotionally and philosophically at the time of the hit-and-run death? Are those ideas and positions clearly shown? Where do they wind up? Can you correlate their changes with events in the mystery?

## ATTACH EACH SCENE TO THE SPINE OF YOUR MYSTERY
Write a one-sentence synopsis describing the action of each scene.
- Does each organically attach to the spine of your book—its premise? Does each involve change to a person, the status quo or the perception of either of those things? Does each scene have internal conflict, opposing pressures of some sort?
- Can you see, by looking at your scene synopsis, that well-developed complications (new information, dead ends, lying witnesses, theories in need of revision, etc.) keep things going or interrupt progress toward the protagonist's goal?
- Are transitions of time and place clear from scene to scene?

107

- What does the sleuth want aside from simply solving the crime? Why this crime? Why the passion for a solution? Are his motives and internal conflicts clear throughout?
- Is the description of character part of the ongoing action—shown, not told? Does it continue throughout the novel, not in inert descriptive globs?
- Does each character want something? What does he do to make it happen? Is what he wants resolved in some way?
- Is everybody necessary? If there's a redundant character with no specific function, or one who could be combined with another with no loss to the story, send him back to central casting to await a meaningful role in another book.
- Does an excess of interior monologue or rumination signal too many solo scenes?
- Does the book begin as close to the climax as possible? What would happen if it started later? Does the reader need to know everything that's up front right then (or ever)?
- Is the scene sufficiently set at the start? Does the reader know, at least in general, where we are—country, city, present, past, future?
- Is setting used throughout to heighten mood and a sense of place?
- Is there a flashback before sufficient movement forward? Wherever you've used one, does it add depth; develop the character; enlighten, heighten, explain and enrich the present action? Is there a simpler way to present that material via immediate action or dialogue? Are transitions into and out of the flashback clear and smoothly handled?
- Is the sequence of events clear?
- Is the point of view established early and maintained throughout?
- Have you avoided coincidence as a solution and built in characters' special skills and potentials early on so their eventual appearance doesn't seem gratuitous?
- Did you play fair—introduce significant characters, including the villain, early in the book and let the reader know whatever the detective knows (even while you directed attention away from its significance)?
- Does the dialogue move the story forward and characterize the speakers in addition to providing information? Does each char-

acter sound different from the others? Does each significant character's speech reflect his psychology and background?

- At the end of the book, are you telling what you already (or could already) have shown?

## PUT YOUR BOOK ON TAPE

After those questions are addressed, read the entire book into a tape recorder. Then, take a deep breath and listen to it. Apply the "gut test": if something in your belly squirms, either upon hearing it or late at night in retrospect, trust your gut. Work on that part.

After mulling these questions (quite possibly more than once) and working on them until you've gotten rid of the kinks and snarls, you're ready to edit for style, for language, for your own voice.

# 18 FINDING YOUR VOICE: THE MICROEDIT

Despite the necessary, painstaking and precise work of polishing your manuscript, style isn't something you should work for, and it's definitely not something to imitate. Your style will appear as you work, developing slowly and on its own like a print in a darkroom sink. As you make your words clear, precise and pleasing to yourself, sweeping away clutter and confusion, you will simultaneously unearth your unique voice, as much yours as your signature is.

Style doesn't mean ornate, verbose, inflated or flowery, and longer isn't necessarily better. It's necessary to mention this because we've been "educated" into bad habits via high school's 500-word essays—not necessarily good words, not necessarily necessary words. We met our quota by inflating our language and using convoluted ways of saying next to nothing, and we were rewarded with As.

Let's look at writing differently, so that clean, swift, economical and vivid prose gets the A—and the contract.

## PARE YOUR MANUSCRIPT

Anton Chekhov, admittedly not a mystery writer, but a good guide all the same, said: "Cut a good story anywhere, and it will bleed." Aim for no fat, no gristle.

Avoid euphemisms. If you mean "dead," don't say "passed on." The same goes for redundancies—e.g., "round in shape," "basic fundamentals"—roundabout expressions, such as "reaching a decision" when "deciding" works perfectly well; and multisyllabic substitutes that add nothing, such as "activate" in lieu of "start."

According to E.B. White in *The Elements of Style*, 3rd ed., *"rather, very, little, pretty*—these are the leeches that infest the pond of prose, sucking the blood of words." Add the word *some* to that list. Let your computer search for and destroy those words and their cousins, like *extremely, rapidly, suddenly, great, awfully*, etc. (A computer search for *ly* will help find them.)

White's coauthor, William Strunk Jr., said:

> Vigorous writing is concise. A sentence should contain no unnecessary words, a paragraph no unnecessary sentences, for the same reason that a drawing should have no unnecessary lines and a machine no unnecessary parts. This requires not that the writer make all his sentences short, or that he avoid all detail and treat his subjects only in outline, but that every word tell.

If you can express the same thing with fewer words, do so.

Remember that all these suggestions apply to your narrative voice. You can use any and all of the don'ts in dialogue to show that your speaker is pompous, vague and incapable of speaking directly or making his meaning clear. But you, the author, don't want to sound that way.

## LOOK LITERATE

Mechanics are fixable, so make sure somebody checks yours. Don't let fear of bad spelling or grammar stop you from writing. Nobody buys a book because its spelling is fantastic. You can pay a professional freelance editor or barter with a friend who is good at spelling, punctuation and grammar if these are not your strengths. (In this instance, your computer is *not* a friend. The functions to check spelling and grammar, as anyone who uses them knows, are fraught with hilarious imperfections.)

## DON'T "TELL" WITH PUNCTUATION

Wherever possible, eliminate exclamation points and italics. They both tell us this is an emotion-laden phrase. Instead, make your narration or dialogue itself show the emotion. Use the computer to search for exclamation points and italicized prose, then decide if you need them.

## AVOID MODIFIER POISONING

"He said angrily" shouldn't be necessary. "He shouted" might do the trick. Or "He spit the words out, as if they tasted foul." Or "With each word, he pounded his fist on the table, making the salt shaker rock." Let the words he said be angry ones. Give him a physical expression of fury. Show, don't tell.

## USE THE ACTIVE VOICE WHEN POSSIBLE

When the subject of a sentence is acting—"Dogs chase cats"—the sentence is active. When the subject of a sentence is acted upon— "Cats are chased by dogs"—the sentence is passive. Passive construction moves in a circular pattern—we first meet the receiver of the action and then find out who is acting upon it and have to mentally circle back. It also almost universally requires more words. Compare "It was brought to my attention by the police officer that Janine was missing" to "The police officer told me Janine was missing."

## USE STRONG VERBS

Go through your manuscript single-mindedly looking at verbs and try for precise, strong ones. You'll add immeasurable life and movement to your writing—and be able to be rid of a great deal of deadwood.

Forms of the verb *to be* are weak—except in Hamlet's soliloquy (he really meant the state of being in "To be or not to be"). In less lofty prose, which is more likely to produce a strong image in the reader's mind? Which tells you what to think and which shows you what you see: "Her hair was beautiful" or "Her hair bounced/curled/gleamed"?

"She was shocked" tells. Instead, find a significant detail to show her surprise. "Her face contorted." "She crumpled into a heap." "She gasped." "She grabbed for her heart medicine." You can depict the emotion in dozens of ways. One will be precisely what you see in your mind, and that's the one that will enable the reader to see it as well.

Other vague verbs include *appear*, *seem*, *feel*, *become* and *remain*. See if you can cut them out and improve the writing. "He felt hatred for her new boyfriend" is not as powerful as "He hated her new boyfriend."

Being specific is harder —but it's worth the effort.

*There is* a common habit of writers. . . . Isn't it better if I say "A common habit of writers is beginning a sentence with the useless *there is* or *there are*"? "There was a corpse on the floor" might become "A corpse lay on the floor."

Again, use your computer to search for *there were/there are/there is* and *it was/is* and see if eliminating those pairings strengthens your sentences.

## USE THE POSITIVE FORM

Instead of "He was not very often on time," use "He usually arrived late." Even a negative is better expressed in positive form: *Dishonest* is an easier locution than *not honest*, and *forgot* is more immediate than *didn't remember*.

## USE PARALLEL CONSTRUCTION

Balanced cadences give your writing some measure of poetry and a definite measure of intelligibility. They can also add humor and memorability.

Listen to how this loses its punch if you take away its parallel structure: ". . . that all men . . . have certain unalienable rights: living, liberty and to pursue happiness."

*Both/ and, not/ but, not only/ but also, either/ or, first/ second/ third*, etc., should be followed by the same grammatical construction. The sides should match.

## PLACE WORDS FOR CLARITY

Remember that one way of hiding clues is by burying them in the middle of a great deal of action and words. In order not to bury your meaning, reverse that. The beginnings and ends of sentences and paragraphs are the strongest. Place what you want emphasized there.

## USE FIGURES OF SPEECH CAREFULLY

Good metaphors and similes dramatize your thought, project its ironies, give it an emotional stance and add poetry, but metaphors that you strain for aren't generally good. It's better to write concrete, un-metaphorical prose than to push for a figure of speech that becomes a howler. Look at these examples of what a reviewer called the "crime of excessive uniqueness." They appear in Bill Pronzini's *Gun in Cheek* and *Son of Gun in Cheek* collections of less-than-stellar writing from, alas, published mysteries.

Silence settled like a hen squatting on her eggs.
Her lips wore smugness like a slipper.
—C.E. "Teet" Carle

Inspiration splattered me in the face like a custard pie.
—Michael Morgan

A good metaphor is economical writing because in very few words, by combining two images, we get a vivid picture, seeing more than the facts alone could convey. It's also accurate. The things compared or equated are genuinely alike. Also, they fit in context and tone. To state the obvious, your medieval mystery can't compare the monk's bright eyes to computer chips.

## USE YOUR SENSES

One of the many lovely things about writing is that the reader never sees the work in progress, and the writer has the opportunity to read through his work in order to consider just one aspect of its rich mix. I've suggested various read-throughs already, but it might be worth your while to read your book again, paying attention to its sensory data. See if you've written for the specific texture, taste, aroma and sound of things.

The correlate to that activity is eliminating the abstract, telling words you've slipped into the story. Describe; don't emote with abstract, imageless and telling words like *gloomy, glorious, charming, frightening*. As mentioned earlier, it is more difficult to be concrete—to honestly express the texture of life, to show life on the page—than it is to pull back and offer up abstractions. The work is worth it, however.

## DON'T HEDGE YOUR BET

Don't back into your sentences. Delete "It seemed like," "It felt like," "It had begun to," "There was"—unless you're writing dialogue for a timid and uncertain person.

Other weasel words that weaken your prose include *sort of, kind of, relatively* (as in a "relatively minor matter"), *unquestionably, necessarily,* etc. Get off the fence—commit.

Another locution that pushes the reader one step away and makes the action less immediate is giving us information secondhand. ("I saw," "She heard"). We're already in that point of view, seeing through those eyes, so don't move us back outside. Go directly to the action. Not "I saw the flash of lightning," but "Lightning flashed." Not "She heard the men arguing," but "The men argued."

## RECYCLING LANGUAGE WON'T SAVE THE PLANET— OR YOUR MYSTERY

*Cliché* is the French word for stereotype, a metal plate cast from a page of type. It's precomputer era boilerplate. Prefabricated, overfamiliar phrases do not produce a mental image. If someone says "a fine kettle of fish," do you actually envision bouillabaisse in the making? Do you envision anything? This gives no sensory input. It's a waste of words and space, as are tired phrases (e.g., *ripe old age, broad daylight, dead drunk*). You know them. So, alas, does everyone else.

## TIGHTEN YOUR TEXT

Instead of "In this room are treasures for which men have killed," use "Men have killed for the treasures in this room."

Make sure everything contributes to the single total impression of the story/chapter. Could anything be thrown away without loss?

Check constructions containing *which, what, who* and *that*. Consider the gains from slenderizing the sentences. For example, in the following, the words inside brackets might be eliminated with no loss except verbosity. "Henry [was a man who] cultivated people in order to bilk them." "[The people that] I want to have you check out [are] the prime suspects." "[What I'm trying to say is] nobody should have been allowed in the crime scene."

## REPLACE TELLING SENTENCES WITH ONES THAT SHOW

Look sternly at any spot in the manuscript where you, the author, have intruded with an explanation, judgment or interpretation. Replace abstract tellings, e.g., "The room was messy," with images. "He'd forged a narrow path to the bed between piles of his dirty laundry." Often, you'll find you've done both—shown, and then told. If so, cut the telling.

## KILL YOUR DARLINGS

"Read over your compositions, and wherever you meet with a passage which you think is particularly fine, strike it out." Samuel Johnson said that, but he didn't mean you should eliminate your fine writing. You should strike the brilliant anecdotes that have no relevance, the line that's so exquisitely poetic and sensitive it fits nothing else in the manuscript and serves no purpose except to flash—in neon colors—the message "Aren't I a splendid writer?" Leave only what works for this story. As Elmore Leonard says, "If it sounds like writing, I rewrite it."

## CHECK FOR VARIED AND APPROPRIATE PROSE RHYTHM

Don't make all sentences long and flowing or short and punchy. Consider a choppier rhythm for great emotion and for your physical and tension-filled scenes and a smoother more flowing rhythm for peaceful segments—the lulls before the storms. The reader breathes along with your punctuation and sentence structure.

## VARY STRUCTURE

Is every sentence subject-verb-object? Does every one (or too many) begin with a descriptive phrase ("Unhappily, she read the . . .," "Moving to the right, she . . .")?

## LISTEN TO YOUR TONE

Have you used appropriate words? "Fragrance" and "odor" are vastly different, and the nuances of word choice for a writer are like those of color choice for a painter.

## CLARITY, SENSE AND CONSECUTIVENESS

Make sure each sentence leads into the next for sense and visual coherency. Become a camera, and record what's seen as it moves. Your camera shouldn't jerk back and forth from outside the house to the inside, from the floor up to the ceiling, then back outside, then into the head of the point-of-view character, then back inside in another room. Move the reader's eyes and mind in a logical sequence.

After you've considered all these things and changed and reread and gotten feedback and reconsidered, put the manuscript down for a few weeks. Then go through it again—and again—until it is as good as you can make it. It's your baby. Give it the best possible start in life.

# 19 TO MARKET, TO MARKET

This book is about writing a mystery, not how and where to market it. Happily, books on these topics—plus annual guides, such as *Writer's Market* and *Novel & Short Story Writer's Market*—are available.

Here we'll briefly discuss *preparing* your work to be sent off to market.

## FINISH YOUR MANUSCRIPT
You did finish your manuscript, didn't you?

With rare exceptions, a first-time writer proves he can complete a mystery by doing so. Later in your career a proposal may suffice, but for now your first job is to finish your work.

## MAKE YOUR WORK LOOK PROFESSIONAL
Once your work is finished, make it look professional. This is not the place to demonstrate your creativity. Conformity is preferred, which translates into black type, double-spaced on white, 8½"×11" (21.6cm×27.9cm), 20-lb. (74gsm) paper. Use easily read type—not script or any other exotic font. Following this format is both a courtesy for the editor's tired eyes and a necessity for the copyeditor, who needs room to make her marks between lines and in the margins (the latter, 1" (2.5cm) to 1½" (3.8cm) on all sides).

Don't bind your manuscript. Mail it with a cardboard backing and secure it with rubber bands.

Number each page and have a header that somehow identifies the work—perhaps your last name and the title of the work, the latter abbreviated if necessary. Put your full address and phone number (include fax and E-mail, if applicable) on a cover page.

Begin the first page of each chapter about one-third of the page from the top.

Always include a self-addressed stamped envelope (you'll see it mentioned in agents' and editors' requests as SASE) with your submission. Be sure it's large enough for return of all materials. (One of the indignities of being writers is that we not only face rejection, we pay the postage for it.)

You can also include a self-addressed stamped postcard on which you have written "I have received Jane Doe's manuscript *A Brilliant Mystery*. Signed, _____. The agent can pop it into the mail, and you'll know your mission's been accomplished.

## KEEP TRACK

Keep records of what you have sent and where it is. *Writer's Market* will give you an idea of the anticipated response time, and if you haven't heard by then, drop a line to the office asking about the status of your work and when you might expect to hear from them. You can give them your phone number, but you could again include a self-addressed stamped postcard or envelope. A letter is less disruptive than a phone call and, therefore, less apt to annoy.

## FIND AN AGENT

As a novelist, you will probably first be in contact with agents, rather than editors. Many publishing firms no longer read unsolicited—unagented—manuscripts, so it's wise to look for representation. This is an arduous task, rather like searching for your one true love; given that this match is based on money rather than pheromones, it's even more fraught. But take heart. Agents are also scanning the horizon looking for their one (more) true love.

Do not query agents who charge a reading fee. The agent you want lives on the faith that your excellent work will bring in revenues from which she'll take 10 percent or 15 percent. For this, she'll market your work to the editor who will be most receptive to your work. She'll negotiate the contract. (If instead, you sell your book directly to a publisher, have an agent or lawyer check the contract before you sign it.) After your book is sold in the U.S., your agent will deal with foreign and subsidiary rights.

You can get leads on agents by attending writers conferences and/ or asking published or represented-but-not-yet-published friends for recommendations. You can spend time in the library with *Publishers Weekly*, an industry publication that often mentions agents and also lists newly formed agencies. An agent building a clientele is doubly motivated to find talent. You can glance through mysteries you enjoy to see if the author has thanked his or her agent, and then research that agent's address in such books as *Literary Market Place*, available at most libraries.

You can learn a great deal about agents from books like *Guide to Literary Agents* (Writer's Digest Books). Find out what sorts of work the agents seek and how much of your manuscript they want as a first glance. (They may want only a letter describing the work, or such a letter plus a chapter, or the first fifty pages and a summary of the rest.) Make a list of potential agents, and see if they accept queries submitted simultaneously to other agents. Many do, and many are accommodating even if they don't say so. Make sure you mention that you are sending this query to several agents, but would give any one of them exclusive reading rights to the manuscript should they so desire.

## THE QUERY LETTER

The query letter is likely to be the most difficult writing assignment you'll ever ever have. You want to say, "Love me, represent me, sell my book today and make me a star!" This is, however, not exactly the way it's done.

Instead, think of why you and your book are unique. Don't exaggerate and don't oversell yourself—the agent's profession is selling. But do mention any special talents or expertise that feed into your book.

Single-space your letter. No one's going to edit it.

Even if you're sending multiple queries, personalize the salutation and be sure of spelling, title and address. Nothing is more off-putting than the sense of being part of an impersonal mass mailing. It won't enhance the agent's opinion of your intellect or style.

This sample assumes that the author hasn't won any writing awards, hasn't ever met the agent, and wasn't recommended to her by anyone. Of course, you'd mention any of that in your letter.

This also assumes that wherever the author found the agent's name, he also learned that she wanted a query letter and the first three chapters plus a synopsis. You don't want to waste postage on mailing the

119

Dear Agent X,

I am an ex-Rockette, a former nurse in Vietnam and an attorney specializing in sexual harassment litigation. After a lifetime of personal experience with variations on the theme of appropriate behavior between men and women in the workplace, I find the questions still unanswered and potentially incendiary.

I have written a thriller that begins with the discovery of the corpse of a prominent politician, found murdered backstage at a Broadway musical. I have used much of my own knowledge of show business, law and men as a basis and background.

My novel *Inappropriate Behavior* provides a tantalizing puzzle, along with torn-from-the-headlines issues of law and power, and the exotic setting of a show. I have enclosed the first three chapters, which introduce the situation and the main characters: Randy Barron, the politician-victim; Veronica Bountiful, the single mother supporting her son by dancing in the show; Allison Briefcase, Veronica's friend and a practicing attorney; and Sturgis Torrid, the impresario charged with the murder of Randy Barron. In addition, I've enclosed a brief summary of the rest of the action.

I am submitting this query to several agents, but would certainly give you exclusive reading rights to the full manuscript should you so desire.

I look forward to hearing from you and thank you for your time and interest.

Sincerely,

entire manuscript to someone who hasn't asked to see it.

If the agent requests a full manuscript, rejoice—and be prepared for an agonizing wait. An agent's job is labor intensive. She can't automate her reading and evaluation, and generally, several people need to read your manuscript and discuss it before a decision is made to represent you. Be patient.

## BE PROFESSIONAL ABOUT IT

Instead of grinding your teeth and obsessively checking the mailbox, let go of that book and begin your next. You've learned more than you realize in the process of writing the first one, so put that to use—and you'll learn even more. It still won't be easy, but now you know it's possible. However, you can't know what's possible until you start writing—again.

Get to it. Your agent and publisher will be delighted to find out that another book is in the works.

# INDEX